Graham M. Mott

How to Recognize and Avoid

SCAMS SWINDLES and RIP-OFFS

Graham M. Mott

Golden Shadows Press
Littleton, Colorado

Although the author and publishers have made every effort to ensure the accuracy and completeness of information contained in this book, I assume no responsibility for errors, inaccuracies, omissions, or any inconsistencies herein. Any slights of people, organizations, books, and newspaper and magazine articles are unintentional. Personal names used as examples in stories are totally fictitious.

Publisher's Cataloging in Publication
(Prepared by Quality Books, Inc.)

Mott, Graham M., 1944
    How to recognize and avoid scams, swindles, and rip-offs /
Graham M. Mott.--1st ed.
    p. cm.
    Includes bibliographical references and index.
    ISBN #0-9633155-0-1

    1. Swindlers and swindling--United States. 2. Fraud. I. Title.
II. Title: Scams, swindles, and rip-offs.

HV6695.M67 1992   364.163
                                         QB192-1676

ATTENTION: PUBLISHERS, WRITER'S ORGANIZATIONS, TEACHERS, SEMINAR LEADERS, BUSINESSES AND CORPORATIONS, NON-PROFIT ORGANIZATIONS, HIGH SCHOOLS, COLLEGES AND UNIVERSITIES: Quantity discounts are available on bulk purchase orders of this book for sales promotions, educational purposes, premiums, or fundraising. Custom imprinting of logos or company name on the cover can also be created to fit specific needs. For more information, please contact our Sales Department, c/o Golden Shadows Press, P.O. Box #687, Littleton, Colorado 80160 or call 1-800-844-7532.

Dedication

To my mother, Aimée G. Mott, for all her thoughtfulness and generosity.

To my wife, DeAnne, who has been such a wonderful friend and companion. Thank you for all your help, editing, creativity, inspiration, support, and understanding.

To my daughter, Kristi, my son, Writer, and my stepson, J. D., for all their cooperation and understanding while I was writing this book.

To my good friend, Ed Seeger, for always being so supportive and willing to go the extra mile for me.

And last, but certainly not least, this book is dedicated to all the people who have lost money to scams. May we all speak out and fight back!

My warmest wishes to you all.

Acknowledgements

I would like to offer my heartfelt thanks to the many people listed below. I could not have finished the book without them.

Adam Wilson is the creator extraordinaire of the cartoons in this book. Thanks, Adam, for giving me just what I was looking for in cartoon characters.

My gratitude to Dona Dodson, Tom Morris, Karen Peterson, Joe Snoy, Susan Yager, Bruce Wiese, Diana Crow, Hal Temple, Jim and Candy Hastedt, Terry, Patti, and Mary Foley, Bob and Wendy Sherr, Paul and Princess Lazotte, and Howard and Jane Jungbauer for all their creative brainstorming as well as computer support.

Thanks to Joe and Judy Sabah and David J. Gruber, authors/self-publishers, for helping to simplify some steps in the writing to publication process. It sure helps to have experienced counsel available.

Table of Contents

PART SIX: The Appendix

Introduction

I have written an easy-to-read book that will tell you everything you need to know to stay free of scams as well as provide excellent advice for those of you who have already been caught and swindled. This book is an important investment in your future well-being as it can save you both money and anguish.

In the following chapters, I am going to tell you my personal story, provide you with detailed descriptions of over 70 different scams, teach you how to recognize a scam and why we get involved, list over 40 agencies/companies you can call for help, information, and complaints, and give you concrete examples, methods, and rules for avoiding scams. (All the stories included in this book are based on actual examples.)

PART ONE
Breaking the Silence

1

Painful Recollections

> *"The true art of memory is the art of attention."*
> Samuel Johnson

•The Impossible Dream•

An unexpected phone call in November, 1991 sent my heart pounding and flooded my mind with memories. The call was from a man who asked if I was a distributor for XYZ Company. He said he had just discovered XYZ's name in the business pages of the phone book under my name and was very surprised to find the company name listed there. He had been told there were no other XYZ distributors in Colorado.

He had recently bought a distributorship from XYZ and had just received his product. He was very excited and enthusiastic about his new business venture but wondered who I was.

•Heartburn•

My stomach sunk. Should I tell him about my terrible experience with XYZ Company or wait for him to discover the truth for himself? I could only offer him cold hard facts and disappointment.

3

•Memories•

I swallowed hard and then told him the story I had been trying to forget. I mentioned that I had 20 years of sales experience and considered myself financially successful. My encounter with XYZ Company was certainly one of the lowest points of my life.

The caller's reaction was total disbelief. He related his story with XYZ. He had invested $4,000. This was more money than his wife knew about. He said he had used up almost all of their savings and thought his wife might divorce him over this mistake. His final remark before saying goodbye was, "I can't believe I could have been so dumb!" When I hung up the phone, I felt sick to my stomach. XYZ had found another unsuspecting victim.

He called later in the week saying he was feeling frustrated and angry. He still had not told his wife the whole story. I tried to offer him some support and assured him he was not alone in feeling betrayed. My best advice to him was to learn from his mistakes and get on with his life.

Our conversation triggered emotions I thought I had worked out. His phone call was like salt on my wound. Obviously, I was still feeling my own guilt over my mistakes and had not worked out my feelings about XYZ Company. I was still incensed over what they had done to me and were doing to so many other people.

•No Man Is An Island•

Having received so much interest from family and friends in my new business venture with XYZ Company, it was impossible to hide my feelings and regrets. I was embarrassed to have to tell my business associates that I had squandered my money on such a foolish and wasted opportunity.

What really surprised me was the secretness behind everyone's failures. No one wanted anyone to know about their poor choices in investments. It was as if speaking of losing money in our society were strictly taboo. Talking about sex, business, current affairs, or our families was far easier than talking about our monetary losses and mistakes. Most people suffered in silence. I found no one willing to share their own experiences until I started telling my own story. I discovered that "misery loves company", and I wasn't the only "fool" out there. Silence was protecting the unethical company by allowing it to continue to perpetuate the scam.

Later, when talking with my wife about the man who had just invested with XYZ Company, I knew that the chapter with XYZ was far from closed. There was a reason XYZ Company kept coming back into my life.

I had kept a journal during my business dealings with XYZ. Now my wife was suggesting that I expand my journal into a book. She felt I could use my own story as an example for others. She believed my own mistakes were the same basic mistakes other people make when they find themselves trapped in a scam. My wife convinced me that my experiences would benefit others and could help many innocent people avoid getting hurt. By honestly telling my story, people would be able to relate to it on a personal level.

•And United We Stand

My story has expanded from a first-hand experience into a first-aid kit for others. I believe sharing it will take the sting out of our mistakes, help break the silence on our failures, and create a flow of educational information to the uninformed. As more and more stories become common knowledge, we can start empowering ourselves and stop corruption from further eroding public faith. We can put our future investments into more honest enterprises.

The event that compelled me to write this book began with a telephone call and ended with a determination to help keep other innocent people from being ripped off. This book is for those of you who do not want to become another scam statistic. It is a composite of everything you need to know to stay free of scams as well as excellent advice for those of you who have already been swindled.

So let me tell you my true story, a painful $30,000 lesson that made me so angry and caused me to write this book........

Next: Reversal of Fortune: The Author's Story

2

Reversal of Fortune: The Author's Story

> *"If we could sell our experiences for what they cost us, we'd all be millionaires."*
> Abigail Van Buren

•Promises, Promises•

In March 1990, I spotted a small advertisement in the classified section of a Denver paper by a company located out of state. The ad stated that XYZ Company was looking for a sales manager to sell a "Hot New Product on the Market." A six-figure income was also mentioned. The ad appealed to the salesman in me. A new product on the market with sizable sales and income potential immediately grabbed my attention. After making a living in residential real estate sales for over 20 years, I was looking for a new and exciting business opportunity. I wanted to change careers. I decided to give XYZ a call to find out more information about their offer.

•Knocking at the Door of Opportunity•

A very friendly fellow with XYZ Company answered my

7

call. I told him I was from Colorado and had just seen their ad in a Denver newspaper. He enthusiastically described a product XYZ had developed for use in fundraising for non-profit organizations. This product was a coupon book offering two-for-one savings on specific items which had wide public appeal. XYZ Company was now looking for distributors to introduce their product into the state of Colorado. They were excited about expanding their business opportunity into several new states. He said other XYZ distributors had found the coupon book highly successful in fundraising activities with all kinds of non-profit groups. These distributors had also discovered that non-profits were looking for new and innovative ways to raise money. He felt the earnings potential was unlimited with the great demand for their coupon books.

He mentioned that in order to represent XYZ and their business opportunity, I would need to purchase a distributorship. As a distributor with XYZ, I would be an independent contractor totally responsible for all my own business expenses. XYZ offered a choice of six different investment levels. I could become a first-level distributor for as little as $800. For the fee, he said XYZ would provide me with a specific amount of coupon books, retail advertising displays, and a sales manual outlining and explaining their sales programs.

Since Colorado was a new state offering all kinds of possibilities, he wondered if I might be interested in purchasing a protected territory so I could be in total control of my own state. He asked if I would like to have the vice-president of sales call me back with more information about a protected territory. My interest was piqued. I said sure, have her give me a call. I was beginning to see the possibilities of being first in Colorado with a new product and controlling my own state.

•**Under The Spell**•

Within 30 minutes, I received a call back. A pleasant woman introduced herself as the vice president of sales of XYZ Company. She was delighted to tell me that XYZ was introducing their new fundraising program into several new states, and no one had taken advantage of this terrific new opportunity in Colorado. She asked me if I was interested in leading Colorado's sales force as XYZ's Major Distributor. I was excited and answered yes.

Since I didn't understand all the advantages of being a Major Distributor, I asked the vice president to explain them to me. She said I would have a protected territory which meant that I would have no competition from any other XYZ distributors. All XYZ distributors in Colorado would be working for me. I would be the only person who could divide up my state into sections and have the right to sell XYZ distributorships for a set fee. There would also be the following additional incentives:

1) I would be purchasing XYZ's coupon books at the lowest price.
2) My distributors would be required to purchase all their coupon books from me.
3) I would be making a profit on every coupon book that I sold to my distributors.
4) I would receive residual or override commissions on all future coupon redemptions from Colorado.
5) I would be receiving the highest residual commissions.
6) XYZ would provide me with all their potential sales or distributor leads for Colorado.

Every coupon book contained a number of redemption possibilities. Each coupon included 10 "buy one, get one free" offers on specific items. There was a serial number assigned to each coupon book which was used to link the distributor to his books. Residuals were commissions paid on each one of these future coupon redemptions from the coupon books. There was no deadline or expiration date for the use of any coupons.

•Jackpot•

If I followed XYZ's plan which was detailed in their sales manual, I could expect to get my investment back in as little as 60 days. The vice president stated that the coupon books sold very well in large quantities because of their two-for-one savings for the user.

Having spent many years in sales, I could immediately see the earnings potential derived from a hot product in a new protected territory. Volume was the name of the game, and I was adding up all the dollar signs in my head. I really liked this service concept and felt this business could be a very creative outlet for me. There was no competition for this coupon book, and the success rate of sales in other states was an indicator of the public's favorable reaction to the product. I was beginning to visualize myself in the fundraising business helping many different non-profit groups.

The vice president told me that I had better make a decision quickly because the company was considering several other people in my state for the position of Major Distributor. The fee for being a Major Distributor was $20,000 while the minimum investment to be a distributor was only $800. XYZ offered six different investment levels for being a distributor. These levels were $800, $1,000, $2,000, $4,000, $10,000, and $20,000. Each distributor level included its own specific incentives for investment. The Major Distributor fee was a very large investment indeed, but it was the only one that would give me the exclusive marketing rights for the whole state of Colorado.

SCAMS, SWINDLES, AND RIP-OFFS

I had caught the dream, a product ripe for the marketplace, that was just waiting to be a winner. I kept thinking how much more money I could make if I was in control of my own state rather than letting someone else purchase the Major Distributorship. It didn't take an adding machine to see the phenomenal dollar amounts that could be earned from large volume sales and all the coupon redemptions. XYZ had created a business opportunity, the "hot" product, and the market demand. Now, all I needed was the money.

The vice president asked me about my business background. Of course, when I mentioned real estate sales, she said I was just the type of person they were looking for to lead Colorado. With my extensive sales background, I would definitely be successful utilizing XYZ's business concept. I told her I would think about it and get back to her soon. Her sales pitch and flattery appealed to my ego. She said that she would be mailing me additional information on XYZ's business opportunity. If I wanted more references, she told me that XYZ was involved with several companies. She gave me some company names and phone numbers.

I had never been in the fundraising business before, but the challenge of beginning something new and marketing an innovative product was very exciting. Suddenly I felt like I had a opportunity to make a difference. If I could provide a means by which non-profit groups could raise money for their causes, I, too, could give something back to society.

I talked to my wife about this new business venture. She could see that I was quite enthused about what I had heard. My wife said that it was my decision to make. If it was something I definitely wanted to do, then I should go for it.

The whole scenario was so perfect. XYZ held a new business in its hand. I felt I was purchasing the whole pie and could slice it up any way I wished. I knew I was just the person to develop it from the start to the finish. It sounded so easy, something I could definitely accomplish, and the potential was outstanding.

•Don't Lead Me Astray•

Because of the large capital investment, I thought I'd better do a little checking into XYZ's background just to make sure this company was as good as it sounded. I called the references the vice president had given me. They were all located in XYZ's home city and state. The only useful information I received from my research was that XYZ had been in business for five years. I found no negative information about XYZ Company.

At this point, I decided to contact some other active distributors of XYZ. I called the vice president and asked her for some names and telephone numbers of other Major Distributors representing XYZ. She gave me the names and numbers of two other Major Distributors located in different states.

•He Spoke Out of Both Sides of His Mouth•

The first man I called was named George. His warmth and genuine interest made me feel as if I was talking to an old friend. He was very generous with his time and information. George told me he loved XYZ's fundraising business and said he was knocking em' dead. He mentioned he had been involved in other businesses in the past, but had never come close to making the kind of big bucks he was now earning. His customers loved XYZ's new coupon book and their fundraising program.

George said the real key was dividing up his state into sections, hiring distributors to sell for him, and leaving time for him to manage the whole program. He stated that he made money by the following methods: 1) selling distributorships for a fee; 2) selling product to his distributors; 3) receiving residuals or overrides on all of his distributors' coupon books' redemptions.

After only one year, George was in the process of taking XYZ's theory one step further. He was increasing his income by dividing his state into protected territories and marketing his own Major Distributorships for $10,000 each. His whole concept sounded so fantastic. I could envision even more profit potential.

George's enthusiasm was contagious. His self-assurance, creative flair, and obvious success convinced me that I had made the right business choice for my own talents. What really appealed to me was George's love for XYZ's fundraising business. He was a superb salesman and a wonderful advertisement for XYZ. (He was the major factor why I decided to go ahead with XYZ's business opportunity.)

Following our conversation, I was even more motivated and excited. I was ready to go full steam ahead. My mind raced with all the new possibilities opening up before me. I was setting up shop in my mind and looking forward to the challenge of creating George's reality in Colorado.

Making an effort to slow down my enthusiasm and momentum, I decided to call a second Major Distributor. He was not as talkative nor as friendly as George, but said he was doing exceptionally well after only six months in the business. He was concentrating on the retail side of the business by placing sales displays for the coupon books in retail stores.

Feeling very confident about what I had heard from both of XYZ's Major Distributors, I called the vice president back to ask her about their corporate training program. She said in order for me to take advantage of XYZ's training program, I would need to travel to their corporate office. The training program would be taught personally by the president of XYZ and would take two full days. The trip would have to be at my own expense. However, XYZ would reimburse me for every dollar I spent in travel expenditures with an equal amount in coupon books which I could later sell to cover my out-of-pocket expenses.

Since I was investing a sizable amount of money in a new career, I decided it was worth spending my own money to visit XYZ for their hands-on training. I made reservations to fly there the next week. The trip would take four days including travel. Feeling enthused, I telephoned the vice president and told her I was planning to visit XYZ, and I wanted to secure the position as Major Distributor of Colorado. She told me to mail XYZ a $500 check as a deposit to hold that position. I mailed the check and was looking forward to my trip.

•Take Me to Your Leader•

In early April, 1990, I flew to the coast to meet with XYZ Company. Waiting to pick me up at the airport was a white limousine. I can't say that I wasn't impressed because I had never ridden in a limo. (As it turned out, this was the only money XYZ Company ever spent on me.) I checked into my hotel in the early afternoon.

The president called me at eight the next morning. He picked me up at nine and drove me in his Rolls Royce to XYZ's office. The president gave me a tour of the office and introduced me to several XYZ employees. The corporate office looked legitimate but was plainly furnished and not particularly impressive. (The office didn't seem to fit with the same image as the limousine, the Rolls Royce, and the success stories I had heard about XYZ Company. I rationalized this with the thought that XYZ was operating a low-overhead operation.) Our meeting began by my asking the president a few business questions. I remember thinking at the time that the president took no personal interest in me such as asking me any questions about my background or family.

•Where Fools Rush In•

Since the training would not begin until I had paid the required $20,000 fee and signed all the proper documents, the president asked if I'd brought a cashier's check. I answered yes. As his secretary was typing up the contract, the first distressing signal reared its head. I was told by the President that my $20,000 cashier's check for Major Distributor would only include one area code (303) and not the other area code (719). Area code (303), which included the metropolitan area of Denver, was composed of the largest percentage of population for the state of Colorado. Area code (719)'s population was much smaller but did contain a viable number of non-profit organizations. The president told me that area code (719) would cost me an additional $5,000 for which I would receive an extra supply of XYZ's coupon books. Because I had only brought a check for $20,000, the president said he would give me a three-month option to cover the additional balance.

To say I was frustrated at the news of an additional area code with increased costs to me would understate my feelings. I thought I was to own the rights for the whole state of Colorado. The president said he was sure it wouldn't take more than a couple of months for me to earn more than enough money to pay off this option. (How I wish now that I had honored that first distress signal and refused to sign the contract. Little did I know that this meeting would continue to reveal new information and new rules increasing XYZ's power over me.)

The president also mentioned that all of XYZ's distributors were required to purchase $500 worth of product every month in order to remain active distributors and continue to receive residual commissions from their coupon book redemptions. I already knew that the distributors I personally signed up for Colorado would be required to buy all their product from me just as I was obligated to purchase mine from XYZ. But what I didn't know was that there was a required amount of product to purchase every month for each distributor including me. Now, I would have to purchase $500 of product per month from XYZ in order to retain my status as the Major Distributor. The president said he would waive the $500 monthly purchase requirement for several months until my business was established. (Suddenly, there were new requirements, more money needed, and no legal counsel available. A dull headache was beginning. I unwisely ignored my inner feelings that I should not proceed with the contract.)

Why did I sign the contract immediately? By nature, I am a salesman. I felt I could take the product and get the job done. I had committed myself before arriving at XYZ Company. My mind was focused on getting the program in action. I had already created business goals for the next year. The roadblocks XYZ mentioned seemed to be only minor detours or setbacks to a very successful business. I signed my name on the dotted line. (What I would find out months later was that I had sealed my fate with a company which was interested only in making money and didn't care about the distributors representing them.)

•School Days, School Days•

The two-day training program began with the president handing me XYZ's sales manual. Between phone interruptions and talking to his stockbroker, the president spent an hour discussing XYZ's business. (I remember feeling frustrated as he seemed to feel it was more important talking to his broker than to me.) He told me he would be tied up in the afternoon so he suggested I go back to my motel and carefully study the sales manual. I was quite unhappy with the news that he would not be available as planned to continue my training. Suddenly, the president's interest in me had faded.

While spending my afternoon studying the sales manual, I was surprised at how poorly it was written. It was very unprofessional. I couldn't imagine showing it to any of my own distributors. My training was certainly not going as advertised. So far, the first day of training had amounted to one hour of discussion and an afternoon of self-directed study.

I was becoming more and more frustrated with the whole situation. The fancy vehicles, modest office, poor training program, and inferior sales manual were all minimized by me. Being on XYZ's turf with their changing rules was intimidating to me. (I was beginning to sense the rumblings of misgivings move from my head to my stomach. My past experiences in sales had acquainted me with difficulties in management so I denied these feelings.)

In talking with my wife that night, she said my voice did not sound good and that I seemed to be discouraged. She wanted to know if I was okay? I said I was tired, but everything was all right. (Since I had paid no attention to my feelings in the past, why would I suddenly start to listen to them now?)

I tried to be optimistic as I arrived for the last day of training. The president spent the morning going over the sales manual with me. He was able to give me a few pointers on how to be successful in their fundraising business. He suggested I lease a small office to make my business appear more professional and use XYZ's name as the name of my own company in Colorado.

To further increase my profitability, XYZ included advertising displays to help market their coupon books. The displays were to be placed in retail stores on a consignment basis. The president stated that many distributors found it very easy to locate these displays in retail outlets due to the fact that XYZ had a working agreement with a specific non-profit organization. The retailer was told that a donation would be made to this non-profit organization for each month a display was located in his store. On this basis, XYZ's distributors found that most retailers were more than happy to accommodate a display and help out a worthy non-profit organization.

•Sour Green Apples•

Finally, at noon of the second day, the president said he was feeling ill and was going home. My so-called extensive training program was completed. He said any questions I might have in the future would be handled by an XYZ service representative who would be assigned to me soon. The meeting concluded with a handshake, wishes of good luck, and the offer to answer any future questions I might have with a direct call to him. My two-day training course had only lasted five hours.

Being quite disgusted with the whole training process, I walked back to my hotel. I spent the rest of the afternoon on the beach sizing up my impressions, I knew on some level that things were not adding up fairly in my favor. I found myself committing more money to a territory I thought I already owned. I was soon going to be required to buy more product each month to ensure my status as Major Distributor. XYZ's training program was inferior to any other training program I had previously known.

The mind can create all kinds of rationalizations. I convinced myself I could overcome all of these obstacles. Challenges in the past had only been stepping stones to my future successes. Nothing was perfect in the world. Why would I expect XYZ to be? (I knew I should have asked for my money back. My feelings told me that the president would never consider returning it. I couldn't see making a scene to try to get my money returned when I had willingly made a commitment and signed the contract. And I didn't want to lose face.)

•Piloting My Own Ship•

After arriving back in Colorado, I could not sweep away my underlying doubts. I told myself that the potential dollar signs far outweighed any negative feelings I had. To bolster my misgivings, I called George. George reassured me I had made the right choice, wished me good luck, and told me to call him anytime with any questions I might have. Before I knew it, he had planted his success story in my head again. I was again humming the Company's tune of prosperity and good fortune. I felt I had a real friend in George.

It was time to get rolling. I leased a small inexpensive office, moved in a desk I owned, and ordered a telephone. I followed the president's suggestion by naming my company using XYZ's name. I sent XYZ a $1,000 check as the first payment toward my option for area code (719). I knew I would be receiving additional product for this payment, but I wanted to make sure I would be the first person to own all of the marketing rights for Colorado.

In the meantime, I typed all of XYZ's business forms on my Macintosh computer. XYZ copies were of poor quality with many mistakes. I could have saved myself money and initially worked out of my home, but from the start I wanted to present a very professional business image. I can now see I was spending far too much money on a program I had never seen in operation. All my money was going out to enhance XYZ's business image, and I wasn't earning any money yet.

My wife kept asking me how I felt about the XYZ Company. I couldn't admit my misgivings to myself, much less to her. Due to my successful sales career in the past, I felt sure I could make this new business venture a success.

•Stung by a Bee•

Now I was anxiously waiting for my shipment of product to arrive so I could start selling distributorships. In mid-May 1990, XYZ's shipment of product finally arrived at my office and included $650 in additional COD shipping charges. (Didn't my $20,000 investment include the shipping costs?) These surprise shipping costs left me feeling angry and frustrated. I now owed additional money I had not anticipated. Nothing had been mentioned to me about any COD charges for shipping XYZ's product. (Could this really be happening to me? Little did I know that the nightmare was just beginning.)

I was livid when I called my service representative. He told me there were additional coupon books included in the shipment to cover my COD shipping expenses. He made all my objections and questions seem crazy. I swallowed hard and paid the COD charges. I was overwhelmed by 25 boxes of coupon books. These boxes filled up almost half my office.

Now, I had another $1,650 worth of untested product which included the $650 in shipping costs plus the $1,000 option payment. (In hindsight, I might have prevented all the future headaches if I had not accepted the shipment, called XYZ, and asked for my money back. That way, I would not have taken receipt of XYZ's product in exchange for my Major Distributor's fee. The contract I signed had specified exactly how much product I was to receive for my investment.)

I could not turn back now. Once again, I dismissed my feelings and forged ahead. Convinced that new businesses always cost more than originally planned, I set to work to develop my own state. If George could be successful, I was sure I could be, too.

•Dangerous Curves Ahead•

Following George's advice, I divided my state into sections based on population so each of my distributors could have his/her own territory to work. I advertised for distributors in the local newspaper and set up interviews. Most of the interviews turned out to be no shows. I eventually signed up two distributors, both at the $1,000 level (XYZ's second distributor level). I trained each of them, joined them on customer calls, and encouraged them as much as I could. A disturbing message that my distributors and I received from non-profit groups and retail owners was their hesitation in doing business with an out-of-state company with virtually no track record and a product that was untested. In conclusion, my distributors could not sell any of their coupon books as a fundraiser, nor could they place the advertising displays in retail establishments.

•Crimes and Misdemeanors•

This was certainly an unexpected setback. But more prophetic was a phone call from my XYZ service representative saying that he had forgotten to mention it before, but he had signed up two new Colorado distributors in area code (303) for me. XYZ, of course, had pocketed the $2,000 in distributors' fees ($1,000 each for both 2nd level distributorships) while I was expected to train these two new distributors. (Was I crazy or was I the one who was supposed to earn the fees for signing up these distributors? Didn't I pay XYZ $20,000 for the exclusive marketing rights for Colorado? Why was XYZ in competition with me? Wasn't XYZ supposed to refer all sales leads to me?)

My service representative reminded me that the major benefit to me was that these two new distributors would be required to purchase all their future product from me. He also assured me that both new distributors were told that I was the Major Distributor for Colorado. He said everything was on the up and up. There would be no future problems.

•Demolition Derby•

Why did I suddenly feel like I had been hit by a Mack truck? I felt like I was going crazy. I didn't know whether to laugh or cry. The joke was unfortunately on me, and I wasn't laughing.

When I called XYZ's two new Colorado distributors, I was immediately faced with their anger. After I introduced myself as the Major Distributor for Colorado, the new distributors expressed immediate disbelief. XYZ had signed them up using the same sales pitch they had previously used with me. The Major Distributorship for the undeveloped state of Colorado was still available. An incredible opportunity for riches could be theirs for only a fee. Even though these two distributors signed up at the $1,000 distributor level, they were told that they could still become the Major Distributor of Colorado by being the first distributor to purchase $20,000 in total product from XYZ. The original $1,000 distributor fee would be credited against the $20,000. Neither my name nor my position were ever mentioned to either distributor. When they called XYZ with a complaint, XYZ refused to refund their money.

My feelings were so vast and deep at this point, I can't even describe them adequately. When I angrily called the president, he told me there had been a communication misunderstanding by his salespeople regarding my status as Major Distributor, and it would never happen again. Being trapped in this business, I knew that I had no choice but to give him the benefit of the doubt.

•Panning for Gold•

In my frustration, I called George, and told him what had transpired. He said nothing like my situation had ever happened to him. I told him I was livid. I wanted to quit the business and sue XYZ Company. George empathized with me and suggested that I concentrate on marketing the coupon books myself rather than worrying about selling distributorships. That way, I could recoup my investment as soon as possible and then get out of the business. This seemed to be very level-headed advice. (The nightmare was only getting worse. My enthusiasm, confidence, and trust were repeatedly being sabotaged by XYZ and its representatives.)

By researching the Denver Yellow Pages, I discovered a potential list of over 150 possible non-profit customers who might be able to use XYZ's fundraising program and coupon books. After my first few telephone calls, to my chagrin, I discovered that XYZ Company had been previously involved in Colorado for the past several years. It was really tough information to hear. One particular non-profit organization gave me the names and phone numbers of several other individuals who had previously been representing XYZ. I called my service representative, and he evaded my question by stating that there were presently no distributors that were active in XYZ's business in Colorado. I knew XYZ had purposely lied to me about this subject in the past.

Family, friends, and business associates had watched and

supported my new business venture. I couldn't admit to anyone that this new business was such a demoralizing and depressing experience for me. I was feeling angry, frustrated, and embarrassed. Since I did not want to lose my total investment, I convinced myself it was just mind over matter.

I set up appointments with at least 20 potential customers. I could not make one sale. However, I almost closed one sale with a large Colorado supermarket chain. Two objections stood in the way of the sale: I could offer no guarantee XYZ would stand behind their coupon books, and I could not provide any references from other companies that had successfully implemented XYZ's fundraising program. When I called my service representative for some references, he used the excuse that these references were confidential information. Now I knew for sure that XYZ had no real references from companies that had effectively implemented their fundraising program in the past. Again, I was faced with more lies.

What I had also come to realize was that XYZ didn't really want any coupon redemptions. The directions for using the coupon book were not easy to understand which made the coupons difficult to use. The coupons were redeemed by mail with payment by personal check, money order, or cashier's check only. Offering a toll-free 800 number and accepting payment by major credit cards would have made the redemptions too easy. Even though XYZ offered savings on these items, the same products were also available locally. People preferred to go out and buy them right away rather than wait three weeks for them to arrive by mail.

•Poison Arrows•

It seemed incredible to me that such a fraudulent company could promote sales without any infrastructure. How could they have developed such a sophisticated con game publicized in national magazines and newspapers, and pulled the wool over so many people's eyes? Didn't anyone ever question their ethics or honesty? How on earth could I have been so blind to such deceit? I had no idea how I would ever recover from this association. I felt totally powerless.

I was beginning to think of a lawsuit. I started keeping a journal on the dates, contacts, and conversations with XYZ's representatives. I thought this could help me in building a case against XYZ. I figured XYZ had committed fraud by selling me a Major Distributorship as a protected territory and then openly competed with me for distributors in my protected territory. XYZ had purposely lied to these new distributors acting as if I did not exist. A lawsuit was the one step I could take that would make me feel as if I was fighting back.

•The Shattered Mirror•

In mid-August, 1990, out of the clear blue sky, I received a phone call from a man who said he lived in Cheyenne, Wyoming. He said he was referred to me by XYZ Company. (Could this be true? Was XYZ trying to do something right for a change?) This man said he was looking for more information about XYZ's business opportunity. He said he hoped to set up a fundraising business in Colorado or Wyoming. I suggested he drive down and meet with me at my office. He said he would stop by the next afternoon.

In the meantime, I heard from XYZ's service representative who told me that I might hear from a man who was interested in the Major Distributorship for Wyoming. (I had to question the prospect's real interest as Wyoming had so little population base.) I told the service representative that this fellow had already made an appointment to meet with me.

The man from Wyoming visited my office and decided that he would be more interested in purchasing a distributorship from me for a territory in Colorado rather than one from XYZ for Wyoming. That way he felt he could work both states. When he left, he said he was sure he would finalize the contract with me for a $1,000 distributorship in a couple of days.

A day later, he called saying he was very upset with XYZ Company. XYZ's service representative had called him and when the man stated that he was going to purchase a Colorado distributorship from me, the service representative told him that under no circumstances could he buy a Colorado distributorship from me. When he argued with XYZ's representative stating that he would purchase a distributorship from whomever he wanted, XYZ's president picked up the phone and told him that his only choice was to purchase one through XYZ's corporate office. XYZ's attitude killed any chance of a sale with this man. He realized that he did not want to be any part of a company that would shaft its own Major Distributor.

I shouldn't have been surprised, but how could XYZ be so unethical and greedy? I was flabbergasted and totally deflated. Feeling sabotaged and helpless, I could hardly make myself get up the next morning and go to my office. I was ready to write off the business as a total loss. I felt sick to my stomach. I didn't know what I was going to do, but I was thinking more and more of a lawsuit.

During the early part of September, 1990, my service representative called to say he was talking to another possible distributor from Colorado. Since he knew I could definitely use some help in hiring distributors, he would like to do me a big favor and sign up another Colorado distributor for me. This time, he would personally make sure there was full disclosure about my position as Major Distributor of Colorado. He knew

I already understood that XYZ would keep the distributor fee.

I only agreed because I thought this might help me if I decided to file a lawsuit against XYZ. I hated the idea of failure. I didn't want to believe that XYZ would intentionally lie to me or other distributors again. (What followed was just the rumbles of a volcano; the eruption would happen very soon.)

Subsequently I phoned this new distributor and was shocked to hear he knew nothing about me. I asked this distributor if he would support me with his story in a possible lawsuit against XYZ Company. His answer was yes. The writing was on the wall: XYZ was only looking out for itself and finding it very lucrative. Once again, XYZ had sold another distributor on the basis of becoming the Major Distributor for Colorado. (How many times does one need to be hit on the head to see the reality of the situation?)

•The Terminator•

I furiously telephoned my service representative with the latest piece of news. My anger fueled his, and we were quickly in a major shouting match. I yelled that I wanted to talk to the president. He said the president would never talk to me again. XYZ considered me a troublemaker. His tirade continued, "We gave you all the tools you needed to be a success. You're the reason that you have failed. Stop being so negative. You're a big boy, so shut up and quit griping." He hung up on me.

When you are attacked, it is amazing how lousy you can feel. I was branded as being negative and a troublemaker. I felt as if I was sinking deeper and deeper in quicksand. At least, I justified to myself, I had never paid the full option of $5,000 for area code (719).

I now realized XYZ's service representative was their tough-guy or hatchet-man. His main job was to defend the company and not give in to any of the demands from unhappy distributors. His duties also included protecting the president by screening all unpleasant phone calls. There was no question that he was the XYZ's intimidator. No distributor, that I was aware of, had ever won an argument with this person. From this moment on, I would have no further contact or correspondence with any representatives of XYZ Company.

•Witnesses for the Prosecution•

During October, 1990, I spent most all of my time investigating XYZ. I discovered 15 previous XYZ distributors in Colorado, who, like me, had never made a sale and were stuck with all their product. The vast majority had invested the amount of $1,000 to purchase an XYZ distributorship. The stories were all similar. Naturally, all the distributors were upset and angry with XYZ. Many had spent their last savings purchasing a distributorship from XYZ and had not recouped any returns on their investment. Most agreed to support me if I decided to file a lawsuit against XYZ Company.

There were four elements which these XYZ distributors had in common. First, they all had heard George's wonderful testimonials. Second, George was the primary reason why each one of them had decided to sign up with XYZ. Third, all of them were sold on the possibility of becoming the Major Distributor for Colorado. And fourth, they all had to face the same intimidating XYZ service representative when they called with complaints and asked to have their money returned.

George had neglected to disclose to me that he had talked to all of these distributors from Colorado. Was it really so surprising that he had never mentioned my name to other prospective distributors interested in becoming the Major Distributor of

Colorado? Perhaps, George's main income was not derived from being a Major Distributor selling XYZ's distributorships and product but rather from being a company man? A commission paid on every sale he helped close would provide him with a very lucrative income, indeed.

•The Underdog•

In December 1990, I received another surprise. A man called saying he found my name (under XYZ's Company's name) in the Denver Yellow Pages. He wondered how I was connected with XYZ Company. Just two weeks prior, he had paid XYZ Company $10,000 and signed a contract with XYZ to be the Junior Major Distributor for Colorado. (A Junior Major Distributorship was the second highest distributor level XZY Company offered.) When I mentioned that I was the Major Distributor, he was almost speechless at the news. XYZ had promised him that he would soon achieve the Major Distributor position when he had purchased an additional $10,000 in product from XYZ. I told him we were both involved in a scam, and there was a strong possibility he might lose his full investment.

I asked him if he had received his shipment of coupon books. He told me that his shipment was arriving the next day. I advised him to find a good attorney, refuse the COD shipment, and ask XYZ to return his money immediately. I also suggested he tell XYZ that he had been in contact with the Major Distributor of Colorado.

He called me a couple of weeks later to thank me for my help and advice. XYZ had refunded his money. I was very happy for him, and pleased that I had played a part in costing XYZ a big sale. Here was another potential witness for my lawsuit.

•The Party's Over•

In January, 1991, I was referred to an attorney who special-ized in fraud cases. We met and I told him my story. My attorney was surprised at my interest in pursuing a lawsuit. He said most people lick their wounds after dealing with a dubious company and don't sue. People don't feel they can afford the legal fees.

Since I had kept very good documentation on my dealings with XYZ and had lined up a large number of witnesses, he felt I had a reasonably good case for fraud. He offered to take my case on a contingency basis which meant he would share in my winnings or make nothing if we lost.

The biggest legal question concerned the wording in my contract with XYZ. The contract stated that if I decided to sue XYZ Company, the suit would have to be tried in XYZ's home state. My attorney felt we should be able to overcome this hurdle. He believed that when I opened an office using XYZ's actual business name that I had established a business office for XYZ Company in Colorado. For the past several years, XYZ had also been conducting business in Colorado which was verified by XYZ advertising for distributors in Colorado's newspapers and by XYZ's previous Colorado distributors. It was to my advantage that eleven former distributors said they were willing to testify in my behalf.

Through further investigation, a local police officer told me that the President of XYZ had previously been involved in a similar scam in a different state. Supposedly when a couple of national law enforcement agencies investigated, he closed up his business, moved out of state, and changed his name. I also called a number of state and federal agencies, both in my state and XYZ's state. The most promising piece of information I discovered was when I contacted a national governmental agency asking if there were any complaints against XYZ Company. I was told a Cease and Desist Order had been filed against XYZ Company in another state. (A Cease and Desist Order stops a company from operating its business in that particular state.) When my attorney requested that this governmental agency send him the records regarding this order, he eventually received a letter stating that all the information had been destroyed and was no longer available.

•Say It Isn't So•

I filed suit for fraud against XYZ Company in January, 1991. This was my last hope to recoup my investment plus all my additional business expenses. XYZ Company hired one of the top law firms in Denver to handle their case against me. During February, 1991, XYZ offered to settle the lawsuit out of court for $5,000. I flatly refused. I was going for all or nothing. It was important for my sense of self-esteem as well as for recouping my losses that I proceeded with my lawsuit.

Unfortunately, in May, 1991, a Colorado judge threw my case out of court stating that I had to bring a lawsuit in XYZ's home state. My only comfort was that XYZ had spent money hiring a high-powered law firm to fight me in Colorado. I was upset but not particularly surprised.

My only other choice now was to sue XYZ in its home state. After careful consideration, I decided that I did not have either the money or the time to proceed with such a lawsuit. Even if I found an attorney in XYZ's state to take the case on a contingency basis, it would still mean the extra expenses of travel, lodging, and meals when I traveled to XYZ's state to testify. All correspondence with my out-of-state attorney would have to be by long-distance phone calls, fax, or mail.

Another major problem was the fact that all my supporting witnesses were located in Colorado. I wasn't sure I could keep a commitment to testify from my witnesses. They might have moved out of town, lost interest, or decided that they just didn't want to be involved anymore. I felt I had carried my lawsuit as far as possible.

I thought it was best to end this chapter with XYZ and get on with my life. I closed my office at the end of April, 1991, and started to look at new employment opportunities. My business and operating expenses totaled $10,000 and included the $1,000 option payment to XYZ Company for area code (719). Adding this $10,000 to my initial $20,000 investment brought my total losses to $30,000. Calling a number of non-profit organizations, I offered my coupon books to them as a donation, but no one was interested. To my dismay, I turned my $20,000 of coupon books and supplies over to a local recycling center in exchange for approximately $35.

•I Can't Get You Out of My Mind•

I am sorry that I am unable to disclose XYZ Company's actual business name. XYZ Company is still selling business opportunities. In fact, I recently spotted two different full-page color advertisements in a major magazine and smaller daily ads in one of the most popular national newspapers. It appears as if XYZ Company has developed a new name, a new approach, and a new product. XYZ is still offering the same business opportunity I invested in, but I believe they are now slowly phasing that one out in favor of their newest venture.

XYZ Company is still abusing unsuspecting people on a daily basis with its glamorous and glitzy business opportunities. While XYZ gets richer and richer, the general public continues to be ripped off.

Next: The Lessons

3

The Lessons

> *"Experience is what enables you to recognize a mistake when you make it."*
> Earl Wilson

•The Facts of Life•

After having read my story, I am sure you noticed most of the errors I made in my business association with XYZ Company. I want to make sure that you do not repeat the same mistakes. I feel it is important to mention them one more time, so here's my list:

☑ **Trust:**
I did not question XYZ's honesty or ethics.

☑ **Expertise:**
I knew very little about the fundraising business and did not do enough research on the subject.

☑ **Legality:**
I did not seek legal counsel concerning XYZ's contract or my legal rights.

☑️ **Greed:**
I did not question the "too good to be true" aspects of XYZ's "golden" business opportunity.

☑️ **Expenditures:**
I spent far too much money on a business with no track record in my state. (The only testimonials came from XYZ's representatives who were located out of state.)

☑️ **Location:**
My communications with a company located out of state were totally dependent on whether they would talk to me and support me.

☑️ **Title:**
I thought purchasing a Major Distributorship would give me a position of power in the state of Colorado and with XYZ Company.

☑️ **Competition:**
I bought a "protected territory" believing I would have no competition from XYZ Company.

☑️ **Sales**
I did not personally check out whether XYZ's product was saleable by showing it to some local non-profit organizations.

☑️ **In Retrospect:**
I see that I invested assets that I could not afford to lose while my pride would not allow me to see all the foreboding signs. Thus the lessons continued to increase and became more painful as my personal power was diminished.

✓ **The most important lesson:**
I would never again purchase another company's business opportunity. I wouldn't give away my power and be reliant on someone else for my success.

Next: The Profile

4

The Profile

"*Experience is the name everyone gives to their mistakes.*"
Oscar Wilde

•Yesteryear's Successes•

My experience with XYZ Company wasn't my first brush with losing money in questionable ventures. My sales career in residential real estate developed in the '70s and '80s. I was one of those lucky people that hit a trend in high volume sales during most of those lucrative years. I became accustomed to large sales volumes and big commission checks scattered throughout the year. Not one to rely on a set or steady income, I developed what some may call a "feast or famine" mentality. Sales offered the exciting lifestyle of a commissioned salesperson with the continuous pressure and stress to regularly produce. With each commission check came the need to repeat my performance. This was not the secure and steady income found in a salaried position which included company benefits. But I liked a "sky is the limit" approach to unlimited income and sales potential.

During the '70s, I started investing in real estate. Housing was continuing to appreciate in value during this inflationary period. I made a wise decision when I turned my investments into rental properties and watched the properties increase in value. My good years meant even more money to invest in other ventures.

•Pressing Your Luck•

In the late '70s and early '80s, I found a new outlet for investing. Not only would it prove to be very profitable, but it would also provide an emotional high for me. This new outlet was Denver's high-risk, high-return penny stock market. Quick profits and few losers produced exciting times. The real estate business and the penny stock market became my work and play routine. With the extra cash, I invested with several different penny stockbrokers. Hyped stocks, confidence, and the right connections produced high profits.

A friend and I met regularly with the stockbrokers and promoters and enjoyed talking about new issues and our successes. We'd buy a stock and sometimes see its value increase as much as ten times or more in one day. Many of my friends and I felt we were on the same roll to the American dream of becoming rich.

I decided to start investing my profits into some bigger investments. Taking someone else's advice, I found myself on the losing side of several oil and gas limited partnerships as well as a multi-level consumer services program. I hit some big winners, but later I lost much of my profits in several other dubious investments. Instead of holding onto my successes and conserving my gains, I continued to play the high-risk investment game. I always had a stronger belief in the other person's ability to make money for me than my beliefs in my own investment and business capabilities.

Coming from those years, I can now see how easy it was. Denver had an exceptional real estate market, the penny stock market was booming, and I was earning much more than I spent. What I was unwilling to see was the reality beyond all those "fun and games" and incredible profits. I could not see the nature of the men behind these ventures. I never really questioned the ethics or the honesty of many of these people or their companies. As I was to learn in future lessons, playing with the high rollers involved very high stakes. In reality, I was just a little guy with a few bucks compared to the big boys. Eventually, some penny stockbrokers and promoters that I knew became names in the news for illegal activities. A high percentage of these new venture companies turned out to be scams. Since I had been making such good money, it had always been easier to overlook that part.

•When the Music Stopped•

Denver's penny stock market eventually collapsed. Suddenly, I was left "standing on the dance floor" with losses in a number of worthless companies. I can now see the quick money I made was really "too good to be true!" I still had some profits left from my penny stock investments. The seed for making fast and big returns on my investments had been sown. The other half of the combination was now missing, the emotional high of quickly making such easy money and big profits. I continued in the real estate business, but my heart just wasn't in it.

•Let Tomorrow Come•

With XYZ Company, I seized the promotion and the excitement of another new creative, money-making venture. I was feeling the natural burnout of 20 years in the residential real estate business and was looking for an exciting new business. I looked into a number of entrepreneurial businesses. I was beginning to feel some real pressure to make a decision and make a break with my sales career in real estate. Feeling restless and looking for a creative outlet, I knew I could be successful in another sales business.

XYZ Company offered a business opportunity I couldn't turn down. I wanted to rekindle those old, exciting, emotional highs. Sales was a part of my competitive nature, and fueled my enthusiasm. Having played the high-risk factor in investing in the penny stock market and finding more success than failure, left me more than willing to take chances again.

•Changing Times•

In the '90s, there is an uncertain economy, a lack of security in the job market, and a dissatisfaction with the pressure-filled fast pace of life. Today's investors aren't as likely to invest on a lark or for fun. Commitment to a new business venture is a more serious matter. Money is tighter, and the losses have more consequences. The possibilities of higher incomes and larger returns on investments have diminished. People are now looking for new ways to increase their incomes and returns on monetary accounts. Many people's incomes are not keeping up with their expenses and bills.

•Batter Up•

The middle class is finding their net worth shrinking. They are seeking other means of making additional money. In some two-income families, people feel they can take a risk with a new investment or a full- or part-time business opportunity because of a second income to depend upon. The easy, free-wheeling deals during a good economy are now developing into a slower, tighten-your-belt economy. With people looking for alternative ways to make money, they are more likely to fall victim to "get rich quick" schemes.

Next: The Formula

5

The Formula

The Company:
•Marketing for Money•

XYZ Company's goal was to make as much money as possible. Their secret to success was high volume sales. XYZ picked an industry the general public could readily identify with in an emotional way. (Examples would include such industries as health, education, sports, recreation, and music.) They then developed a fresh approach with a new product which would fit a particular need in that industry. XYZ packaged this product into a business opportunity. This business opportunity would provide large profits with low overhead expenses. XYZ needed a product which would: 1) be inexpensive to produce; 2) create immediate cash sales; 3) provide repeat orders; 4) cause no liability suits; 5) have relatively little competition; 6) demand future redemptions providing residual or override commissions.

•What Does It Cost?•

XYZ marketed their business opportunity by selling distributorships. A distributorship was the vehicle used by XYZ to earn money. It was important that XYZ set a specific dollar value for purchasing each distributorship. XYZ's minimum investment level of $800 needed to be within the affordability range of a large percentage of Americans. The second investment level was only $200 more or a total of $1,000. XYZ was shrewd and offered enough additional incentives so that new distributors would prefer to spend $200 more and buy a distributorship at the $1,000 investment level. Plus, XYZ offered the right to purchase a protected territory or the incentive of earning it through additional product purchases.

XYZ Company's potential earnings from sales of distributorships were very high as can be seen in this example:

25 sales a week @ $1,000 each equals
$25,000 per week or
$100,000 per month or
$1,200,000 per year
50 sales per week equals,
$50,000 per week or
$200,000 per month or
$2,400,000 per year
100 sales per week equals,
$100,000 per week or
$400,000 per month or
$4,800,000 per year

•Targeting the Public•

XYZ's goal was to attract the investor from middle class America. They targeted a wide segment of the population promoting the following types of opportunities: 1) full-time; 2) part-time; 3) two-income families; 4) retirement; 5) single parent; 6) supplemental income; 7) a home-based business.

•Decreasing the Liability•

In order to decrease XYZ's liability and avoid potential lawsuits, XYZ Company followed two important criteria. First, they delivered a specified amount of their product for each distributor's fee. In this manner, they provided value for payment. Second, XYZ made sure it conducted its sales campaign and all of its business out of state. This made it very difficult, inconvenient, and expensive for anyone to bring legal action against them.

•Creative Promotions•

Promotion was the real key for XYZ. Their campaign highlighted quality, value, and service. The cunning marketing of XYZ convinced the individual that he/she was on the cutting edge of a dynamic new industry. Emphasizing the great timing of this growth opportunity, XYZ produced a product with little liability in an area without much competition.

The key element for XYZ's venture was promoting their product. They needed to convince the public that they were offering something of value and meeting a consumer need which had not yet been met. Appealing to the American dream of financial independence, they designed their campaign to have strong identification with earnings, success, prestige, and security.

•The Brochure•

XYZ spared no expense in creating and developing a very professional and visual sales brochure. The company's brochure contained a large number of endorsement letters from clients. There were also graphs and charts describing the potential market for the product as well as tables showing exceptional income projections.

Also included were two, full-color ads. One showed a successful distributor clearly illustrating the profits to be made with XYZ's program. The second ad showed XYZ's product with easily recognizable brand names that were available through redemptions from the coupon book.

This brochure was the only visible means of seeing the company's operation unless visiting XYZ's offices at one's own expense. Even when visiting, one would only be shown a small part of their offices as there would be no signs or any mention of its extensive telemarketing operation.

•Developing the Sales Personnel•

The single most important factor in marketing the sales program involved XYZ's sales personnel. Well-trained, friendly, warm, and upbeat in their sales approach on the phone, XYZ's telemarketers promoted the success of XYZ Company. If XYZ's sales personnel could not close the sale, they referred the prospect to an officer of the company. After speaking to the officer of the company, it was often suggested the prospective distributor contact one of XYZ's successful out-of-state distributors. These individuals hyped the program with rags-to-riches tales and promoted the virtues of the company's business opportunity. These so-called, out-of-state distributors were probably collaborators on XYZ's payroll. In the majority of cases, their testimonials were all that was needed to finalize the sale.

•Spreading the News•

XYZ spent the majority of its budget on its promotional and marketing campaigns. XYZ promoted its business opportunity with half-page and full-page ads in national magazines as well as carefully planned, smaller ad campaigns in local and national newspapers. XYZ wanted to pique the potential prospects interest with its advertisements, thereby causing them to initiate the first call. In this way, XYZ had already found an interested prospect. XYZ captured the prospect's interest by stating that they had: 1) a new business opportunity; 2) a hot new product; 3) great earnings potential; 4) new territories now available.

XYZ's priority was, first and foremost, selling its business opportunity. After the sale, XYZ's follow-up and support were basically nonexistent. XYZ's promotion convinced the general public that it had the program and the product to help them achieve financial success and wealth.

•It's a Bird, It's a Plane, It's a Scam!•

XYZ's success was derived from its ability to sell the program rather than from developing an outstanding business opportunity and product. Basically, XYZ provided an idea loaded with propaganda, incentives, and a title for an $800 fee. The product received was of questionable merit, and the business/sales manual provided little help in implementing a grass roots business. The reality of the whole situation was that while XYZ was becoming rich, its distributors were unsuccessful in marketing their business opportunity and generally lost all of their investment.

In summary, XYZ's formula for success included:
1) Establishing a need;

2) Developing a product;

3) Determining a cost of the product to the distributor;

4) Selling an attitude such as, "you can be very successful" or "you can get rich quickly;"

5) Getting a commitment or closing the sale.

The Prospect
•Sweet Nothings•

The potential prospect was attracted to XYZ's business opportunity for the following reasons: 1) the high income potential including residuals or override commissions; 2) a new product; 3) no competition; 4) a new market area; 5) the ease of doing business; 6) a training and support program.

•A Case for Investing•

Marketing XYZ's venture offered the prospective distributor the following: 1) a full- or part-time business; 2) outstanding income potential; 3) being an entrepreneur or his/her own boss; 4) low overhead working out of his/her own home; 5) earning income right away; 6) hiring and managing a sales staff; 7) an opportunity to own a protected territory and be a Major Distributor; 8) a service-oriented business helping non-profit organizations.

•Great Expectations•

Most prospects signed a contract after talking to one of XYZ's successful distributors. Later, these people discovered that they had absolutely no idea how to market or implement XYZ's fundraising sales program. Further erosion of their confidence came with each potential customer's rejection.

A large number of investors felt as if it were their fault that they could not market XYZ's business opportunity. If they called the company with any of their doubts, they were assured by XYZ's representatives that it was totally their problem. The embarrassment that these distributors felt about their mistakes was something they only wanted to forget.

•Hard Realities•

The majority of XYZ's distributors were stuck with all their product. Many held on to their coupon books hoping for some opportunity to sell a portion or to find some other way to recoup their losses. They did not know they had been conned or that they had purchased a concept which was not fully developed or supported by XYZ. If they figured out that XYZ was selling a scam, they still felt powerless.

With XYZ located out of state, the consequences of legal action became complicated and expensive. If they wanted to file a lawsuit, attorneys' fees would have cost far more than their distributors' fees. In the end, most of these distributors took their lumps, caused no problems for XYZ, and were never heard from again.

As the following projected sales figures will show you, the potential income as an XYZ distributor looked excellent but was really minimal when compared to XYZ's potential earnings.

Each distributor hires two salespeople.
Each salesperson sells 2 customers a month
= 4 total sales a month.
1000 coupon books sold to each customer at $10 a piece
= $10,000 total profit

x 4 sales per month
= $40,000 total gross sales per month
= $20,000 gross profit to non-profit customer
= $20,000 gross profit to distributor
 - $10,000 for inventory and sales commissions
= $10,000 distributor's net profit per month
x 12 months
= $120,000 distributor's net profit the first year.
$.50 paid on each redemption
x 40,000 possible redemptions
= $20,000
+ $120,000 distributor's net profit
= $140,000 distributor's total first year's income

XYZ made millions of dollars in a year from their distributor program while XYZ's distributors earned little or no money at all from the sale of their coupon books.

Next: Are You a Prospect?

PART TWO
A New Scam is Born Every Minute

6

Are You a Prospect?

> *"One who thinks that money can do everything*
> *is likely to do anything for money."*
> Hasidic saying

•The Most Wanted List•

Are you a likely prospect for a scam? Absolutely no one is immune from scams. You may have already been taken in by a scam, or you may think you are too smart to get rip offed. Don't necessarily bet on it. Chances are, you are going to hand over some of your hard-earned money, from $30 to $1,000 to $10,000 to $50,000 or more, to some stranger you hardly know. And you are going to be happy to do it and thank the stranger for this wonderful opportunity. You'll never see your money again. When you discover you have been ripped off, you are going to be so angry, ashamed, and embarrassed that you can

hardly talk about it. You will feel foolish and utterly powerless. Here you allowed this stranger to dip into your pocket. Worse yet, you helped put his hand right into it and allowed him to take your money!

We all want to believe that scams only happen to others. Virtually everyone is a potential prospect for a scam. In reality, it has touched some of the most successful and educated people in our society. Doctors, lawyers, professors, CEOs, famous actors and actresses, professional athletes, and millions of others have all been victimized. The educated, wealthy, and sophisticated are taken in just as easily as the poor and uneducated. Special interest groups such as senior citizens and foreign immigrants seem to be hit the hardest.

Scams are like a wild fire, totally out of control with no rain in sight. Every facet of our society is being affected by this growing malady. The '90s are seeing this epidemic of scams dramatically increase. It is estimated by the North American Securities Administrators Association that scams could cost us between $40 and $50 billion each year. We don't know the true estimate of losses incurred by scams. Due to the silence surrounding these losses, the actual figures total up to more than double the projected figures of $40 to $50 billion. Telemarketing, health, and insurance frauds total over $100 billion in losses alone![1] Money that could have been spent on legitimate products and offers is being lost to fraudulent investments. Siphoning good money into bad investments by questionable means continues to undermine our national economy.

•Lightning Does Strike Twice•

Many times, the prime candidates to be rip offed are those who have been involved in a previous scam. Hoping to recoup their losses, people take unnecessary risks. Most losses are in

[1]"Health Care Fraud," U.S. News and World Report, February 24, 1992, 34-42.

the range of a few dollars to a few thousand dollars. Because of the smaller amounts of money that are lost, few people report their losses, file complaints, or seek legal aid. Legal aid can cost more in time, money, and emotional strain than is worthwhile. It is much less costly to ask for legal advice before you make a mistake than afterwards. Losing larger sums of money can be so embarrassing to people that their embarrassment and shame far outweighs their desire to do anything about the loss.

The number of victims continues to grow. Many of you think that you are the only ones who have lost money in such a foolish manner. Fearing criticism from family and friends, you refuse to talk about your mistakes. When the pain of being cheated is significant enough, you will begin to fight back.

Are you a candidate for a scam? To find out, turn to Chapter 19, page 169, The Questionnaire: (A Risk-Taking Probability Quotient).

Next: A Dictionary of Scams

7

A Dictionary of Scams

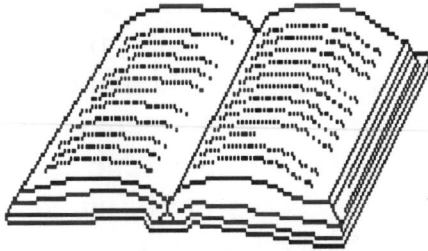

scam, n. "a confidence game or other fraudulent scheme for making a profit; to cheat or defraud, a swindle, swindler, swindling" (The Random House Dictionary of English Language, Second Edition, Unabridged, 1990, New York).

•Dangerous Liaisons•

There is no way to mention every type of scam. I have included as complete a list as possible. Scams run the gamut from purchasing water purifiers to investing in gold mines. Many times, these scams are based on the newest products in the medical, health, and other fields. The more popular the product is today, the better it will probably sell to the public. People hear about these new products and are usually interested in giving them a try.

Remember, I am not condemning all companies and/or their products. There are many reputable and honest businesses. But no business is immune from being used as a scam. This list is to alert you to the areas where abuse has taken place. When making a choice, you need to be as analytical and careful as possible in your decision-making. **Caution is the keyword! Become a critic-at-large.**

Listed next are examples and explanations of various types of businesses which have been found to be operating unethically:

•2nd Mortgages•

You are sold on the idea of investing in second mortgages on commercial and residential real estate properties. High interest rates are promised. You are not told that other lenders are not interested in these loans due to poor credit risks. And some of the properties may have more than one second mortgage on them already. These mortgages may be unrecorded leaving you no legal recourse or chance for recovering your investment.

Also beware of "easy-to-get" second mortgages. You could borrow against your home's equity to use for home improve-ments, a vacation, a college education, health care, or a new car. These loans can have front-end fees, high interest rates, prepay-ment penalties, and balloon payments. You could be approved for a loan where you can't afford the payments and eventually lose your home to foreclosure. **Be skeptical, don't pay any money in advance, check out the lender, ask for references, and talk to your own business advisor, banker, or attorney.**

•14-Karat Gold Jewelry•

There seems to be a large supply of gold jewelry on the market. Much of it is fake or of poor quality even though it is stamped "14 karat." Make sure there is the manufacturer's registered trademark or monogram next to the 14-karat symbol. Both the trademark and the symbol should be the same size.

Just because it is a good deal doesn't necessarily mean it has any value. Your best bet is to buy from a reputable jeweler. Also beware of fake gemstones and watches. **Know your seller.**

•800 Long-Distance Numbers•

These phone numbers are toll free. When you call some 800 numbers, you may get a recording which tells you that in order for you to receive information regarding what prize, gift, or vacation you have won, you must access another number by using your touchtone phone. This new number may be a costly 900 number. Be on the lookout as this technique is being used for many other scams including sweepstakes or prize give-aways, employment, credit, etc. **Just because you are calling a toll-free 800 number, be on the lookout for other ways you could be charged for the call.**

•900 Long-Distance Numbers•

These are generally recorded messages costing many dol-lars per minute, and the charges add up quickly. These numbers provide useless or worthless information on almost any type of subject including "how to get rich, how to start your own business, how to do home improvements, numerology, astrol-ogy, tarot," etc. 900 numbers are big money-makers for the owners. Many companies advertise their 900 numbers on cable TV. Due to so much fraud with these types of numbers, some phone companies are no longer offering new 900 numbers. Consumers can dispute 900 number calls and charges under the Fair Debt Collection Act. Check with your local phone com-pany. **Do yourself a favor, save money by never calling a 900 number!**

•Business Opportunites and Franchises•

All these opportunities appeal to the big money you can earn, how easy it is sell and use the product or service, and how

quickly you can start earning income. You may be told that
there is not much competition for the product or opportunity.
Many companies sell you the product and then forget about you
since they only care about making the sale. Beware of companies selling you useless programs or products. Just because the
company advertises in a well-known or reputable magazine, it
doesn't mean the company won't take your money and run.
Think Scam.

•Cable Television Advertising•

The cable television industry is growing very rapidly because the advertisers can reach such a large audience. There are
more and more "infomercials" on cable television especially
on late-night television.

In many cases, you think you are getting an endorsement
from the person hyping a product when it really is an advertisement. These productions have fantastic visual sales techniques
which grab the watcher. Some are so slick and professionally
produced that you think you are watching a regular television
show. They have a paid studio audience cheering on the
presentation. And there may be a well-known personality
giving testimonials for the product or service. Quite a few of the
claims and promises can be deceptive and misleading. The sale
usually includes some item or items that will be sent free along
with your order. Payment is by credit card.

The Federal Trade Commission regulates these infomercials
by requiring the company to put a disclaimer on the screen
notifying the audience that they are watching a paid television
commercial.

Again, be wary, as you are vulnerable to this kind of visual
advertising. If you place an order, you may never receive the
product and if you do, it won't be worth what you paid. **Watch
out for these video and audio delights. Don't let your eyes,
ears, or wallet get too carried away.**

•Canadian Lottery or Lotto Group Program•

The premise is that you have been specially selected for entry in a special group program which has increased your odds of winning. You will share the winnings of your group. All you have to do is send in a check or call using your credit card to enter.

•Cellular Telephone Lottery•

This involves a phony premise putting up money to enter the FCC's lottery for cellular licenses in rural areas in order to construct cellular telephone cells. You are guaranteed almost a 100% chance of winning. You don't win anything. **This is not prevalent like it was in the past, but with new types of communication coming soon that require federal licensing, keep your eyes and ears open.**

•Chain Letters or Pyramid Schemes•

These are phony "get rich quick" schemes. These offers eventually fail because they quickly run out of people. **Tear up all these offers.**

•Collectibles•

These include items such as fine art, gemstones, stamps, coins, sports cards and sports memorbilia, jewelry, etc. The general appeal is the great value of the collectibles. You are told that you should be able sell these collectibles for a quick profit. Most are fakes or have little or no value compared to what you invested. Make sure you require and obtain a written certificate of value or authority from a reputable appraiser, preferably of your own choosing. Ask for company references and financial statements. **Don't let the "Greed Factor" grab you!**

•College Scholarship Services•

There usually is a front-end fee or advanced payment fee required. Don't pay until the service is provided. The company will state that there is a scholarship already set aside for your son or daughter, who is so deserving because he/she has an excellent school record. **Flattery is nice but don't believe these promises!**

•Counterfeit Lottery or Lotto Tickets•

A person tells you that he/she has a winning ticket but cannot cash it as he/she is an illegal alien (in the country illegally). He/she agrees to split the winnings if you will give him/her one half of the winnings in cash before you cash in the winning ticket. The ticket is counterfeit. **Only purchase lottery or lotto tickets from an approved outlet.**

•Credit Card Merchant•

These scams can occur with smaller businesses that want to become a credit card merchant being able to accept credit card charges. A front-end or advance fee is charged, the service is never provided, and the fee is gone.

•Credit Card Schemes•

The con man will use any method he can think of to obtain your credit card numbers so he can make unauthorized charges on your card. **Never give out your credit card, checking account, phone card, or any other personal account numbers. When using your card, don't let anyone peek over your shoulder and see your card's number.**

•Credit Repair•

These firms offer to repair your credit problems or your credit report for a fee. You can call your local credit bureau to get a report on your credit file. Call your bank to find out the name and phone number of the local credit bureau.

•Death in the Family or Obituary Bible Con•

Shortly after a loved one has passed away, a bible is delivered to the home with an exorbitant COD charge. Never accept the COD charges on any unknown packages.

•Direct Debit from Checking Accounts•

The salesperson asks for your checking account numbers and bank information so that he can use this information to have your payment directly debited from your checking account. Then he withdraws funds from your account using printed counterfeit drafts that look like your real checks. You could have unauthorized withdrawals against your checking account. Carefully check your monthly bank statements. **Keep your checking account information private.**

•Discounted Mortgages•

You are promised higher than normal returns on your money by buying, selling, and trading discounted mortgages or "paper." Companies may use sales seminars to sell this type of investment.

•Dirt Pile Schemes•

These are found primarily in California where investors pay a lower price for supposedly unmined gold in the ground.

•Employment or Job Placement Services•

These companies circulate resumes and mailing lists of so-called excellent job opportunites. They make a fortune using 900 long-distance numbers. They may run legitimate looking job ads in the classifieds of your local newspaper (an example would be for "Public Relations or Advertising Executive"). These teaser ads get you to call for information making a long distance call on a 900 number.

These rip-offs may also include guaranteed foreign employment opportunities. When you call the company, the position is always filled. If you call on a toll-free 800 number, the company sells you on paying them an up-front fee. For that fee, they guarantee to find you a job. Once you've paid your money, there is little recourse. **Kiss your payment goodbye.**

•Environmental Products•

These products include items such as water purifiers, air purifiers, radon kits, etc. The appeal here is to protect your family's health and improve the environment. You overpay for a product that really doesn't do much. **Read all the information carefully. Don't get carried away.**

•Equity-Skimming Schemes•

This is a newer type of fraud. What is most threatening about these types of scams are that they can cost you your home as well as your credit ratings.

This may appeal to homeowners who are in financial difficulty and need to sell their homes quickly in order to avoid possible foreclosure. The seller is promised by the con man that he will take over the payments, and will share any leftover equity with the owners when the home sells. After the homeowners sign over the deed to the house, the con man rents out the house, never assumes the loan nor makes any payments, and eventually foreclosure proceedings are started against the owner. (When it involves signing over your equity, many states have a three day right of recision so the owner can change his mind. For more information, call your own State Attorney General's office.)

Some con artists suggest they use a real estate contract which states the sale is "subject to a rehabilitation loan." This clause allows the buyer to go to a lender and borrow money using the seller's equity as collateral. The buyer borrows the money, and the sellers end up owning and owing on a new mortgage.

Also, if there is a large amount of equity in the property, the scam artist may talk you into borrowing against this equity in order to make an investment. **Don't sign any papers without first getting legal advice. Always protect your equity.**

•Exotic Bird or Animal Farming•

This can involve ostriches, emus, llamas, etc. You are asked to invest and promised high returns with a company located out of state. **Be suspicious of these kinds of investments.**

•Expensive Perfumes•

These perfumes are usually inexpensive fakes. Is the salesman representing a reputable company?

•Fake Cancer or AIDS Cure Clinics•

These clinics promise miracle cures. Many clinics are in Mexico or other countries, tend to be very expensive, and do not have cures.

•Found Your Pet Hoax•

This is one of the cruelest scams. The con man plays on the pet owner's emotions by calling to say he saw their ad and has found their lost pet. All the owner has to do is to send him a specified amount of money, and he will send the pet home. **Agree to pay a reward only when you have received your pet.**

•Free Baby Photographs•

Here a company offers free baby photographs but pressures you to purchase expensive photo packages. If you only take the free photos, there will be an expensive service charge.

•Free Vacations, Sweepstakes, or Prize Giveaways•

These types of scams continue to be very prevalent in the '90s. These unsolicited offers usually arrive at your home on a postcard or in an official looking envelope promising you a free prize or vacation. In most cases, you are required to make a large purchase in order to receive your gift or trip. (An example would be having to purchase a six-month supply of vitamins or skin care products.) A call back on an expensive 900 number may also be required. The value of the products you purchase is small compared to the high price you pay.

Remember, the vacation is not free. There will be restrictions and extra hidden costs for these so-called "free vacations." Also, the free prize you have won is not what you thought it was and does not have much value. If you are interested in an offer, ask for more information in writing regarding all rules, restrictions, and exceptions. Very carefully make your choice. These offers are better off in your trash. **Take a deep breath and keep yourself under control.**

•Fundraising, Non-Profits, and Religious Schemes•

These companies may use words in their names such as "AIDS", "Cancer" or any other cause which is highly popular today. (Examples would be phony sales pitches by the supposedly disabled.) These appeal to your emotional need to help some worthy causes.

Also watch out for phony Christian fundraising drives and animal shelter sweepstakes saying you have won a prize if you will give a donation. Make sure you know your religious, charitable, or non-profit organizations before investing. Do not hesitate to write or call for information about non-profits to the agencies listed in Chapter 15. **Ask for the non-profit organization's externally audited financial statement and annual report.**

•Grocery Coupon Rebates•

This opportunity is presented as an easy money-making business where you can work out of your home. All you have to do is clip grocery coupons and a company will pay you up to 50% of the cash value of all the coupons you send to the company. The company charges you a fee to get involved in this business. You are either paid a much smaller percentage than promised, or you never receive any money for your work.

•Health Products•

These could include weight loss programs, arthritis remedies, baldness products, vitamin and mineral supplements, skin care products, nutrition schemes, AIDS relief medications, rogaine-like hair replacement products, Chelation Therapy with EDTA, Candidiasis Hypersensitivity (fungus), and any health, facial, or body creams that supposedly contain Retin A (a prescription product). The appeal is to stay healthy and young. Usually, the price will be far too high for what you receive in return. These products usually do not work. Be careful of all newly advertised health products. **Don't waste your money on these products.**

•Health Care Fraud•

Older Americans are especially susceptible. Be wary of calls promising free health checkups or health tests. Never give out your social security number, Medicare number, medical history, insurance numbers, or sign insurance forms for strangers. Check all your health-care bills carefully. Be suspicious of anyone trying to sell you on health-care services or equipment you may not need. Con men are using other people's insurance and medical information to charge the government billions of dollars in fraudlent claims. **Just because someone treats you nicely, doesn't mean you should necessarily trust them. You don't know their motives.**

•Home-Based Businesses•

These are very popular with more and more people wanting to work out of their homes. The appeal is staying home and making easy money with low overhead costs. These companies sell you on their ideas and products. Once they sell you their money-making program and products, you get no more help and the business fails due to inferior products and materials. **Get as many references as possible and check each one out thoroughly.**

•Home Improvements•

There are over 10,000 traveling workers who travel around the U.S. soliciting home improvement jobs. Many are con artists who will not hesitate to take your money when you aren't looking. These workers may be found where there has been a disaster caused by hail damage, flood damage, tornadoes hurricanes, earthquakes, etc. They usually come door to door but could advertise using a brochure or an ad in a local newspaper. Don't let these people in your house without first checking their references and don't pay for materials before the work is completed. These workers won't hesitate to use high pressure sales tactics. After they have completed their work, make sure you check all your window and door locks as they could have unlatched a window or door and later come back to burgarlize your home. Be on the lookout for free furnace or roofing inspections, exterminator services, and foundation or driveway repairs. Always get a second or third estimate or opinion on the necessity of repairs and the costs of those repairs. **Beware of the "door-to-door" home improvement sales-man or handyman!**

•"How To" Brochures, Manuals, or Tapes•

These are sold by mail order and cost you a fee, offer a

money-back guarantee, and have a central theme about getting rich. (Examples: "How to get rich, How to work at home," etc.) Once you pay your money, there is little chance you can get it back.

•Insurance•

Scams are prevalent in health, auto, life, and all other types of insurance. This is a major problem because policyholders are being defrauded by unscrupulous insurance companies, and insurance companies are being conned by dishonest policyholders. Insurance fraud already costs billions of dollars in losses, and the numbers are increasing rapidly. Some examples are false injury claims, faked auto accidents, premeditated car theft or damage, etc.

Many claims also involve fake health insurance scams selling senior citizens supplemental health insurance policies. If you receive a worthless policy, you may not find out until you have a claim. Some may use your name and information to send fake bills to Medicaid and receive the payments in your name.

•International or Overseas Telemarketing "Boiler Rooms"•

As laws become much tougher and restrictive, more and more telemarketers go international but have local mail drops so that you think they are legitimate U.S. companies. Calls to these companies could be expensive plus there is no legal recourse against them.

•Jewelry Sales•

In this business opportunity, you purchase a certain amount of fashion jewelry and displays in advance. You are sold on how easy it will be to get your displays placed in retail establishments. You could be stuck with worthless product and displays.

•Loan, Credit, and Mortgage Brokers (Advance Fee or Front-End Fee Loans)•

These types of scams are one of the most widely used frauds of the '90s. They offer loans or promise credit to distressed businesses or individuals by charging exorbitant up-front fees or advance fees which are non-refundable. You never receive your loan and lose your fee.

Consumers may be guaranteed credit cards. (Some cards may require that you only purchase items from a catalog of overpriced items.) Companies take lengthy credit applications over the phone using a long-distance 900 number which cost the consumer many dollars in telephone charges. In the majority of cases, the customer receives a worthless card or no credit at all.

Also watch out for individuals or phony mortgage loan brokers who sell you on reducing the term and the interest on your home mortgage by having you make your mortgage payments to them. (These are called bi-weekly mortgages or other mortgage acceleration schemes.) Companies charge high advance payment fees, and are supposed to make the monthly payments for you to your mortgage company. (Remember, you can accomplish the same thing by paying an additional amount toward the principal on your own mortgage each month.) Do not hesitate to talk to your own bank or mortgage company first. These unscrupulous companies take your money, make only part or none of the payment to your mortgage company, can cause you foreclosure problems, and hurt your credit rating. **Caution is the real keyword.**

•Look-a-like Government Envelopes or Stationery Promotions•

These look very similar to government standards or are duplicates of government agencies stationery and envelopes.

They may have a picture of an eagle, the White House, or some other governmental symbol on them. Write and ask for more information and references.

•Magazine Subscriptions•
These are normally offered for some special, low subscription rate. Some salespeople are so slick that you do not even know that you have purchased a subscription until you receive the bill in the mail. Often, the invoice is for hundreds of dollars for multi-year subscriptions, and it may be difficult to get out of the contract.

Another premise is offering several free magazines subscriptions. However, there is always a catch such as having to pay only a few dollars each week as a service fee that really totals to many dollars a year. **Hurry and hang up the phone.**

•Mail Order•
Most of these companies advertise a specific product, but what you get was not what was advertised nor has any real value. Some examples of these types of products would be "bug grabbers," baby toys, small appliances, games, etc. Most promise money-back guarantees. Don't believe these promises. Watch out for mail order companies that use direct mail or classified ads. **Know your company, read all the information, and take your chances.**

•Modeling Agency or Services•
These sell you on the dream of making you a model or star. They take photos of you and sell you on paying for a full page of pictures in their modeling magazine. The cost is high, and the promises are false. **Through your own investigation, find a first class agency.**

•Money Manager or Financial Planner•

These use the premise that they know how to make you money by investing your money in various investment opportunities. **Get as many references as possible.**

•Multi-Level or Network Marketing•

As multi-level businesses become more legitimate, it gets much harder to tell which ones are fraudulent. The unethical ones sell you on the fantastic income you can make by selling the product or service to large numbers of friends and acquaintances who will also sell it to many others. All the people you sell and all the people your customers sell become part of your downline, and you receive a commission on every sale. These companies hope you can sell a few of your relatives, friends, and neighbors. The product is really secondary and only a means to making big dollars. In order to get involved, you are required to either purchase the product or pay a distributor fee. Most people get caught by the "greed factor" but never make any money. These fly-by-night companies make millions and disappear with your money. **Watch out for the "How much money you can make theme" with no real emphasis on the company, its products, or its services.**

•New or Used Electronic Equipment?•

Here, you are offered new equipment at cheaper prices. Make sure you open the box and inspect the equipment carefully to make sure it does not look refurbished. Also make sure the manufacturer's warranty and instruction booklet are included. **If you don't know the seller, you take chances with the quality and age of the product.**

•Others Memorizing and Using Your Phone Card, Credit Card, or Cash Debit Card Numbers•

Always be cautious when using your credit cards at airports

and train stations or anywhere large crowds are present. Do not allow anyone to look over your shoulder to see your card numbers or let them hear you give your card number verbally.

•Overseas Employment Opportunities•
These businesses guarantee overseas employment for a one-time front-end or advance fee. This service is sold promising glamorous opportunities, excellent pay, tax benefits, and paid living expenses. **Don't believe any job guarantees.**

•Pay Phone Schemes•
This business is advertised as easy money. Some may even guarantee a certain income per pay phone. Most do not back up their promises to find good locations. And sometimes, the phones may never be delivered or may be in poor condition.

Also be suspicious of private pay phones located in public places such as airports, hotels, etc. The charges for using these phones can be very expensive. **Before using the phone, dial "O" and ask about the rates.**

•Penny Stocks•
Avoid these types of stocks (listed at $5.00 and under in the pink sheet listings) and especially blind pool stock offerings. These types of companies and offerings are now under much tougher restrictions and are much less prevalent. **Scams are now appearing in stocks that are priced just over $5.00 and listed on the Nasdaq over-the-counter stock market.** These are the two criteria that exempt stocks from most of the required rules used to stop penny stock fraud. **Investors beware!**

•People Impersonating Government Officials•
If a person comes to your door stating that he/she is an IRS, Medicare, Social Security, or other government official, ask for his/her credentials and call to verify who he/she says he/she

really is. (Normally these government officials do not call on you personally. You are required to go to their office.) **Call the proper governmental agency to verify that this is how they are conducting their business.**

•Phony Currency Exchange Schemes•

These use the premise that you can purchase foreign currency at a discounted rate. Then the currency will be sold later at much higher rates of return giving you a large profit. **Don't believe it.**

•Phony Foreign Banking Schemes•

Due to the instability and insolvency of many of our banks and savings and loans, people are more intrigued with the possibilities of depositing their money in foreign banks. These foreign banks offer high rates of return on the premise that they are not governed by the laws of the U.S. government. The funds could disappear as soon as they are received. **Be suspicious of anyone selling you on the idea of international banking.**

•Phony Yellow Page Advertising Invoices•

Small businesses are the primary victims. The Yellow Pages logo is not copyrighted or trademarked. Phony Yellow Page bills, invoices, and charges could be sent to your business demanding payment. **Don't pay if there is any doubt as to whether you owe the money. Verify all charges.**

•"Pigeon Drop Con"•

This is one of the oldest con games. The premise is a stranger approaches you showing you that he/she has just found or is carrying a large sum of illegal cash. Sometimes, he/she pretends to be a foreigner or illegal alien. He/she may not trust banks. If you will help him/her deposit, launder, etc. the money, he/she will share the money with you. In most cases, you will be joined by an accomplice who also offers to help.

There are a number of different variations to this con game, but you are always asked to withdraw a large amount of money out of your account to cover the others' shares. When you do, you are left "holding the bag" which is empty. **Don't let your "greed gland" get you too excited!**

•Political Contributions•

These supposedly represent the political candidates or their parties. Check out each one carefully before giving any contributions. **Ask them to send you financial information and references.**

•"Ponzi" Schemes•

These sophisticated schemes are used with almost every kind of investment opportunity. Here the company pays its previous investors a return on their investment with new investor's money. That way the older investors keep referring new customers to invest in the fraudulent company. Generally, all the investors lose in the end because the whole scheme eventually collapses.

•Precious Metal Investments•

These guarantee "to good to be true" returns from the investment in gold or other high grade metals. Some may even be bank financed with the investor only having to put up a portion of the investment.

•Promissory Notes•

This is an investment scheme guaranteeing higher than normal annual returns by purchasing one-year promissory notes. The notes are sold through a private fund. Profits or proceeds from the notes would then be used to make trades in more traditional markets. This could work well as a "ponzi" scheme paying older investors with new investors' money. **If it sounds "too good to be true," don't take any chances.**

•Public Fax Machines (credit card activated)•

These companies sell you Fax machines promising fantastic returns. They promise to place the Fax machines for you in excellent public locations. The appeal is the ease of making big returns on your investment. The machines and locations may never materialize.

•Purchasing Counterfeit or Stolen Merchandise Cheaply•

The counterfeit items can be purchased at retail stores or flea markets. Almost any kind of well-known products including watches (examples: brand names such as Rolex, Gucci, Cartier, etc.), clothing, perfume, music cassettes, movie videotapes, and more are available. The products are of inferior quality and not worth much.

The con man may also let you know he has stolen merchandise, and it can be purchased cheaply. Generally, you do not receive what you thought you would, and you overpaid for the item.

•Real Estate•

These personal, wealth-building programs show you how you can become rich by buying and selling real estate with little cash and low risks. These progams are sold by infomercials or seminars. You pay for the "how to" information or for attending the seminar. People may give testimonials to help sell the program. Most people do not make any money. Plus, unless you are very knowledgeable and careful, you could lose money on your future real estate investments. Talk to a competent real estate broker about your local real estate investment market.

•Repair Schemes•

These can involve both small and large appliance repairs (at-home and in-store) and also can include automobile repairs. Ask for references or personal referrals. **Get second opinions or estimates.**

•Sales Seminars•

These free seminars can cover virtually any product, business, or investment opportunity. You may be sent complimentary tickets in the mail. Also, as a sales incentive, you may receive a rebate check which you can use as part of your payment should you decide to invest. The sales hype and testimonials provide the incentive to pay your money and sign up on the spot. Keep your cool, never sign a contract at a seminar, do not provide any personal information about yourself, and take plenty of time to check out the opportunity. **Don't worry about missing out on a "fantastic" offer.**

•"Scavenger" or "Revenge" Scheme•

This is where an unscrupulous company feasts on an unwary prospect for the second time. The premise is the con man contacts you by phone or by mail to say that he knows you lost money in a previous scam. Now a group of other unhappy customers have united together to either investigate or bring a lawsuit against this unethical company. The con man asks you to help out by paying a certain amount of money to help with the legal expenses. This is a tough one to turn down as it appeals to your need to seek justice and possibly get your money returned. Ask for the phone numbers of others involved as well as the number for the company or firm heading up the operation. (You don't have to pay any legal fees to be part of a class action suit.) **Hold on to your money.**

•Self-Liquidating Loans•

The premise is to receive credit points for every person you get to join the organization or purchase its sales program. You will then be eligible to receive a specialized loan that you never have to pay down. All you pay is an up-front fee as a commission to the organization. No qualification is required. The loan is promised to have a low interest rate, a long-term payout, and can be renewed for a fee. **Look out for the "how easy it is to obtain this loan" sales pitch. Does this offer sound "too good to be true?"**

•Small Businesses Offered Free Prizes•

Free prize or vacation giveaways are the premise for these scams. In order to redeem the prize, the small business owner is told he/she must purchase so many dollars of promotional items (ex: ballpoint pens, baseball caps, etc.) When the business owner receives the promotional items, they are of inferior quality, have little value, and no free prize ever arrives.

•Stocks, Bonds, Funds, Gold and Silver, Oil and Gas Drilling, Mining, Real Estate Investments, and Limited Partnerships•

The key here is to know who you are talking to about these investments. Check out the company's reputation as these tend to be larger monetary investments. These companies promise or guarantee high returns and low-risk investments.

This investment could be a "ponzi" scheme with the company paying you with new investors' money and asking you for additional money and referral customers, and eventually disappearing with all your money. Make sure any limited partnership is registered with the proper governmental agency such as the Securities and Exchange Commission (SEC). **Think rationally.**

•Tax, HUD, FHA Refunds•

This is an employment scam promising job seekers a finder's fee for locating the people who are to receive these refunds. It requires you to pay a fee for a list of supposedly eligible prospects who may receive a refund from the federal government. You have to pay all of your own business expenses for making these calls. You would contact the eligible people on the list and be paid a fee for each one you informed about the refund. After the work is accomplished, the company will not pay you any of the promised fees.

Also beware if you are contacted as a possible recipient of one of these refunds. Do not pay a finder's fee before receiving your refund.

•Television "Air Time"•

This investment offers you "air time" on cable and low power television stations. You are told you can double or triple your money because the "air time" is going to be sold at much higher prices to people who want to advertise their products.

•Timeshare Resales•

These schemes guarantee to sell your timeshare unit for an advance or front end fee. Your timeshare never sells, and your fee is gone. Don't pay before the service is provided.

•Unclaimed Government Funds or Assets•

These offers use advertisements stating that there is unclaimed money waiting for you in the U.S. government's vaults. You call a 900 number and pay a fee for the information on how to obtain these funds. The company guarantees to give your investment back if you do not receive some money. Do not make the call, give out your credit card number, or send a check. If you mailed information about unclaimed funds, it is useless.

•Vending Machine Sales•

These companies sell you vending machines with big promises. They advertise using well-known snacks and soft drinks. They also guarantee to find you great locations for the vending machines but do not come through. This market is very competitive with most of the best locations already taken. These companies sell you on how easy this business is, how you can earn money by just working a few days or hours a week, and how you can start earning money right away. Many times, you end up being stuck with the vending machines and all the product. **Nothing is that easy.**

•Very Cheap Long-Distance Phone Service•

These may be off-shore operators located in the Caribbean. The cost will be more than you think. A front-end fee may be required to start the service. The service is either poor or not really available.

•Very Cheap Quality Name Brand Products•

Be especially careful as these products are generally "too good to be true."

•Wireless Cable•

This new business transmits cable television programs by microwave towers to home antennas. The scheme is to sell you (for a fee) on the opportunity to obtain a license to have the right to use this new technology. The licenses are awarded by an Federal Trade Commission's lottery drawing. The investor is not told about the risks nor is given all the information. Telemarketers are now soliciting investors to help purchase equipment and to build wireless cable systems while promising low risks and big returns. **Look out for the new technology crazes.**

Next: The Con Man

8

The Con Man

> *"I never met a con man I didn' t like."*
> Unknown

•Attracting Your Attention•

Don't look at that friendly, smooth-talking salesman as a harmless guy just trying to make a living. He may be disguised as a good guy but in reality he's a villain. His only motive is to get his hands on your money, and he will use every means at his disposal to get it. Sales are his game. You and your disposable income are his prospects. Winning is the ultimate high for this trickster.

The con man understands that people buy for only one reason: emotional satisfaction. The more immediate the gratification, the faster the potential prospect will say yes to his offer. He believes it is easier to promote an existing desire than to create a new one.

Getting your attention in whatever manner possible is the con man's need. He will solicit you by phone or send you magnificent offers through the mail. Not stopping there, he will advertise a needed service with a 1-900 number to call. That call, of course, is at your own expense. The con man will spend more money on commercials, buy more space for magazine

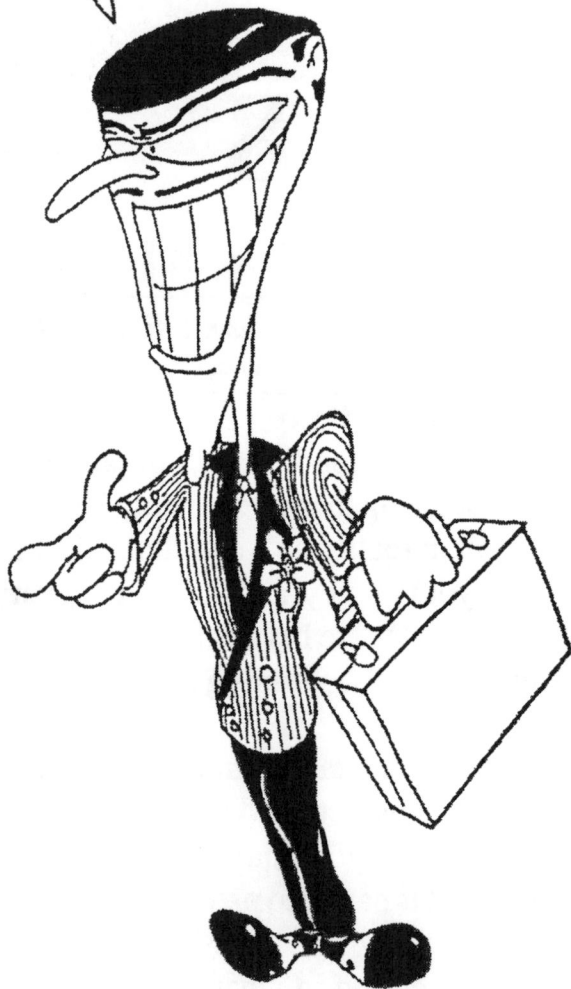

advertising, and send more junk mail than you can imagine. He will outthink, and outlast any objections.

The con man knows the subtle art of manipulation. Almost everywhere you look, you may find the artful disguise of the con man camouflaging a sophisticated scam. He has gone through many ego-bruising battles in order to learn his trade. With true gusto, a compelling drive for the big bucks, and an inability to accept the word no, he is a formidable foe in the world of business.

Patience and diligence are essential for the con artist in seizing an opportunity and setting his game plan in action toward his goal of obtaining cash on the line. Through the school of hard knocks, he has learned the value of quickly sizing up the potential customer. The con artist has discovered that fear, curiosity, easy money, and pride get his prospect's attention. Aggressively, he pursues his customer until the sale is finalized.

The con man of today is a sales pro who memorizes his sales pitch well. Being very persuasive, he inspires confidence. Whether talking to you in person or by phone, the con man attracts your attention by getting on a first name basis with you. He makes you feel as if he is an old friend or good buddy. He is a master of small talk and an excellent listener. The con man can mold you like putty as he closes the sale. Playing to your emotions, he usually leaves you feeling very good and wishing you could talk to him again.

Enormously versatile, the con man answers objections to his sale before his prospect has even thought of them. Cleverness is the con man's second personality. He is aware that an excited prospect will seldom raise any objections. He knows when to turn on and off his charm, when to act upset or show frustration, and when to put on the pressure. He usually is several steps ahead of his prospect.

The con man realizes that the sale generally happens in the first five minutes, or he may not make it at all. However, the longer he can keep you talking, the better chance he has of eventually closing a sale. He is exceptional at overcoming any objections and by deftly changing the subject, you may not even realize it has happened. By asking carefully planned questions, he is able to manipulate the conversation until you end up asking to close the sale yourself.

•Promises Not Kept•

Con men usually promise a large profit potential with very low risk when selling their scams. These swindlers have no intention of honoring their promises. The one thing they have in common is that they will tell you virtually anything to talk you out of your money. They are first-rate actors ready to convince an unsuspecting target of their genuineness. They will confidently put your hard-earned money into their bank accounts and leave town without a trace. The only evidence that con men leave behind is a history of their scams.

(In the above descriptions of the con man, the "he" gender has been used. The phrase was used only as method of description. This is in no way meant to convey that all con men are male. Females fit the description just as well.)

Next: The Set Up

9

The Set Up

•Total Exposure•

There are an estimated 275,000 businesses in the U.S. selling products through telemarketing. They earn over $183 billion per year.[2] Since telemarketing reaches virtually every home in America, many unethical companies also use and abuse the system.

The majority of the telemarketing firms are ethical, but these percentages are rapidly changing as more and more new ones are looking for ways to make a fast buck. Unfortunately, the bad companies are only hurting the reputations of the good ones. The disreputable firms are intentionally committing fraud using the telephone.

If a telemarketer is legitimate, he will be glad to answer all your questions and provide you with all the written material and references you ask for to back up his claims and promises.

[2]Kremer, John, 1001 Ways To Market Your Book, 1989, Ad-Lib Publications, Fairfield, Iowa, 204.

•The Name Game•

Telemarketing companies are often found in warm climates with beaches and palm trees. Such states as California, Florida, Arizona, Nevada, and Texas have been very popular locations. Because of the advantages of developing a "boiler room" operation, new telemarketing businesses have now opened in every state. Many of these companies use patriotic or governmental names such as "United, State, Federal, American," etc. as part of their company's name to make it seem more legitimate.

These companies tend to hire very young salespeople whom they can easily teach their telemarketing methods. Young people find they can earn much more money in this illegal business than they could in other legitimate businesses. Quite a few telemarketing salespeople move on to open their own "boiler room" operations.

•A Piece of Cake•

Telemarketing is such an easy way to reach the general public. The cost of setting up a "boiler room" or "phone room" operation is very cheap compared to the potential return on the investment. All that the operation needs is to: 1) lease an inexpensive office space; 2) have a bank of phones installed; 3) set up a long-distance service; 4) hire salespeople; 5) write sales scripts; 6) purchase mailing lists of potential customers.

The many advantages for a company to use telemarketing to contact the public are:

1) A salesperson can reach more prospects faster.
2) A salesperson can separate the "suspects" from the "prospects".
3) A salesperson can determine a "prospect's" need before his call.

4) Telemarketing can save on the cost of transportation.

5) Telemarketing can save time in travel and waiting.

6) Telemarketing can save wasted time from cancellations.

7) Telemarketing makes it easy to market the product anywhere.

8) Using east-west time zones can expand the selling period.

9) Exterior weather is usually never a problem.

10) A salesperson can use sales scripts and take notes.

11) All the information a salesperson needs is at his fingertips.

12) Phone calls often get instant attention.

13) A salesperson can get right to the point without offending anyone.

14) A salesperson's appearance is not important.

15) Any physical handicaps of the salesperson will not interfere.[3]

Next are two examples of successful telemarketing scams:

A man in New Jersey received an official-looking letter which had a window in the envelope showing a check. When he opened the letter, there was a check for $7,500 made payable to him. To receive his money, all he had to do was call a 1-900 number. He was very excited over his good fortune as he was unemployed. He didn't read the fine print on the back of the check. He called the phone number and was kept on the line for over 20 minutes talking about himself and answering questions. Several weeks later, he received a large number of consumer coupons which were his real prize. And to his dismay, he later opened a phone bill for his 900 number call. This bill was for over $119 since this call was billed at $5.95 per minute.

* * * * * * * * *

[3] Ley, D. Forbes, The Best Seller, 1990, Sales Success Press, Newport California, 84.

A woman in Mississippi received a phone call from a friendly man who stated that she had been picked to receive five nationally known magazines free for the next year. He told her that sales of these magazines were slow in her area so this was a very special offer. All that would be required of her was to look over the magazines, read the articles that interested her, look at the ads, and show them to her friends. There would be a small service charge of only $2.97 per week to cover the postage and handling. She thought it sounded like a wonderful offer and agreed. Soon she started receiving some of the magazines. Then a bill arrived in the mail for over $150 to cover the service charge. She was quite upset as she was not aware of the actual cost, but felt she had no choice but to pay the bill.

* * * * * * * * *

These are five questions you can use to help you recognize or detect telemarketing fraud:
1) Is the caller pressuring me for a quick decision?
2) Is the caller refusing to mail me additional information?
3) Is the caller refusing to give me references?
4) Am I required to purchase additional items in order to receive the offer?
5) Am I required to pay an additional amount in order to receive the offer?

If you answer any of the above questions with a "yes" answer, this is a very strong indication that the offer is fraudulent. A "yes" answer should turn on your radar signal immediately. This danger signal not only tells you to beware but also to make sure you avoid the offer. Take no chances!

Next: The Approach

10

The Approach

> *"Reasons that sound good are not the same*
> *as good sound reasons."*
> Unknown

•As American as Apple Pie•

There are many types of scams disguised as money-making opportunities offered to investors. Hiding behind respectability, these companies present an all-American image. They create a feeling of "family" through their sales approach. Promising communication, support, service, and dependability, they sell their prospects on being a member of their winning team. Upbeat and positive, these companies promote the vision that they are a "perfect company."

•Picking on the Private Investor•

People are much more vulnerable to a scam than they would actually believe. Appealing to the innocence and trust in every person, the con man picks areas of vulnerability. Targeting money markets, the con artist zeroes in on people who invest their money in various ways to increase its value. Those receiving lower interest rate returns on their money are prime candidates for scams promising high returns with low risks. People who talk regularly by phone to their investment counselors are more likely to be candidates for investment frauds. The con man has a ready audience for talking about new investment opportunities with someone already familiar with the investment market. Once he has established a common interest with his prospect, he is on his way to making a sale.

Successful scams may be based on newly advertised products. Health care products, medical aids, environmental safeguards, etc. are new markets for scams. More and more scams are advertised in popular magazines and major newspapers. These periodicals only sell advertising space and have neither the time nor the money to investigate the quality of their advertisers.

Telemarketers flood the mails and phone lines with all types of offers and free prizes and place phone calls to thousands of people each week. Some people may receive as many as three or four mailings or calls per week. People who choose to read this junk mail are more susceptible to this type of seductive advertising.

Did you know this information about junk mail?

✓ It is estimated that Americans receive approximately two million tons of junk mail, but only read half of these mailings.

✓ The U.S. Post Office earns 20 percent or more of its total earnings from junk mailings.[4]

✓ Each year a person will receive an average of 216 pieces of direct mail and 50 phone calls from telemarketers who contact 7 million persons a day.[5]

[4]Allen, Eugenie and Fretts, Bruce, Forbes 1992 ExecutivePage-A-Day Calendar, Workman Publishing Company, New York, NY, July 1, 1992.

[5]Ibid, September 5, 1992.

•Bulking the Mail•

Telemarketers are able to purchase specific mailing lists targeting many different ages or income brackets. They know the quickest, easiest, and most direct method of tapping the reservoirs of surplus income from carefully surveyed polls of what particular groups of potential customers like and dislike. Their sales scripts are carefully written to appeal to certain groups such as senior citizens or retirees. Almost everyone in America is on someone's mailing list. These mailing lists sell cheaply considering the large list of potential prospects. Promoters mail out millions of cards or letters using such slogans as "Open Immediately," "You have won the Grand Prize," "Extremely Urgent," etc. The mail may resemble official government mail, telegrams, or even look like an official check.

Cards sent to prize winners may require a call back at the caller's expense on a 900 long-distance phone number while others may give a toll-free 800 number. The prize winner may be required to make a purchase of some kind in order to receive the advertised prize (ex: overpriced vitamins or face creams). Many times, the prize may not arrive or is not what the winner expected.

Food for thought about 800 and 900 phone numbers:

☑ Toll-free 800 numbers can triple the response rate from direct mail offers. Orders are received a week or two faster than by mail.

☑ Normally an 800 number call produces larger orders because of the phone salesperson's opportunity to interact with the customer. Toll-free 800 numbers encourage much more impulse purchasing by customers. People who purchase by phone tend to be better credit risks.[6]

[6] Kremer, John, 1001 Ways To Market Your Book, 1989, Ad-Lib Publications, Fairfield, Iowa, 28-29.

☑ Movie stars, music stars, professional athletes, professional wrestlers, race car drivers, etc. use 900 numbers to generate income. For instance, the teenage rock idols, The New Kids on the Block, made over $30 million dollars in two years with over $4 million of the total coming from 900 number calls providing recorded information about their personal lives.[7]

•Preferred Payment•

Most telemarketers prefer payment by credit card. Upon receiving approval of the charge, the payment quickly transfers to the company. Some unethical companies may use your card for unauthorized charges or cash withdrawals. If you have a question regarding any of your charges, you should notify your credit card company immediately. **There is no time limit for reporting unauthorized charges when someone else has illegally used your credit card.** Make sure you specify that it is an **"unauthorized charge"** on your credit card as some companies may treat it only as a billing error which has a completely different set of rules.

The Fair Credit Billing Act allows you to contest any billing errors in writing within 60 days of the billing. This would include any product that was misrepresented when you purchased it. In many cases, there may be no interest charges on the item in question during the 60-day investigative period. Ignore any promises of quick refunds from the company with which you have the dispute (refunds usually never show up). These companies have ways of stalling to make sure your complaint is not settled within the 60-day grace period. Always check with your credit card company first as to its policies, rules, and regulations.

[7]Kremer, 51.

How about these facts on credit cards?

✓ Americans own more than one billion credit, debit, and ATM cards.[8]

✓ Credit card holders generally have better credit histories, greater household incomes, and more disposable income than others.

✓ Credit card customers tend to spend more on each order. Credit card holders are much more likely to buy by mail. Accepting credit cards makes it much easier for customers to order merchandise and also to pay for their orders.[9]

✓ All Visa Card numbers begin with the number 4. All MasterCard numbers start with a number 5. All Discover Card numbers lead off with the number 6.

Beware of anyone calling to verify your credit card numbers and asking if your card starts with a specific number. The real motive of the caller is to have you give him your full card number so he/she can use it for unauthorized charges. Ask for his/her name, company's name and phone number and call back to complain to a supervisor.

5 Steps to Take to Protect Your Credit Card Numbers

1) Make sure you carefully destroy or shred all written correspondence about your credit cards including bills or statements, pre-approved credit card applications, pay stubs, and checks. If your monthly credit card statement fails to arrive on time, contact the issuing company immediately. (Con artists will not hesitate to go through your mailbox or trash to obtain your credit card numbers.)

[8]Allen and Fretts, September 12, 1992.

[9]Kremer, 50.

2) Make sure you ask for and destroy all carbons and sales slips from any use of your credit card. (This would include all purchases, rental car agreements, travel itineraries, ticket receipts, hotel bills, etc. If you keep these receipts for tax purposes, carefully file them away and shred them later at an appropriate time.)

3) Make sure you refuse to write your address or phone number on any credit slips or your credit card numbers on your personal checks. Do not allow anyone else to do so also. (This practice is against many credit card companies' regulations as well as illegal in some states such as New York.)

4) Make sure when using a personal identification number or PIN that you pick a number to use that is not obvious. (Do not use your birth date, address, telephone number, or consecutive numbers.)

5) Make sure when using your calling cards, you cover or shield your cards as well as the phone so no one can see what you are dialing.

6) Make sure you do not give your credit card number out over the phone. (The exception to this rule would be if you are ordering an item and feel comfortable about the company with which you are doing business. There is always some risk.)[10]

Currently, there is a new fraud used to bilk the consumer out of his money offering a simplified method of payment for items. Upon ordering an item, the company informs you that they can accept payment only by an automatic withdrawal from your checking account. They ask you to give them your bank name and address as well as your checking account number. The fraud occurs when this withdrawal is followed by unauthorized cash withdrawals from your checking account using counterfeit checks that are similar to yours.

[10] Schultz, Ellen E, "Credit Card Crooks Devise New Scams", The Wall Street Journal, July 17, 1992, C: 1,2.

A word to the wise: Be very careful and keep all your personal financial information private!

Next: The Factors

11

The Factors

•Having It All•

There are two major reasons Americans seem to be easy marks for con games. The first reason is the great American dream. Americans believe that everyone has the opportunity to become rich and successful. Immigrants coming to America heard that the American streets were paved with gold. "Gold in them thar hills" echoed in the West, and the legendary tales of the "oil barons" fueled the belief that this was the land of opportunity.

Americans think that the good life is within everyone's reach. Along with the dream of becoming rich is the desire to drive a luxury car, own a beautiful home, take wonderful vacations, and keep up with the Joneses. Many times we are envious of what we don't have. "The grass is always greener" syndrome has its roots in the American dream. Our society is caught up with having possessions. These possessions define who we are through others' eyes. We have a great drive or need to make money and be successful.

•The Joker Is Wild•

The second reason we respond to a con artist is that we believe in luck and good fortune. We are bombarded with all kinds of contests and sweepstakes telling us that we have an opportunity to win a prize. Numerous states have adopted a lottery or lotto games. Still more are approving legalized gambling. Even though the odds of winning are very small, we want to believe that we can win something whether the prize is big or small. We all look forward to the thrill of winning something free. We identify with the advertised winners as we can visualize winning, too. We love the thrill and power of being a winner.

Why does a scam work? Here are three basic factors why we find scams so appealing.

•Licking Your Lips•

"The Greed Factor" is the single most important clue to understanding the tantalizing emotions we feel when we connect with a sales ploy. We feel excited hearing such words as "you can earn over $100,000" or "you have won a free vacation to Hawaii."

We can visualize making money or taking a free vacation Everyone wants something for nothing. **We feel a real rush or a high as if our "greed gland" has secreted its own special kind of adrenalin.** The greed factor has hooked us right from the beginning. We feel as if we can't miss or are on to a sure thing. This is when we are most vulnerable "to being led down the garden path." The salesperson, ad, or offer is so persuasive that we are ready to sign up on the spot. It is especially difficult for us to step back, think rationally, and keep the proper perspective on these types of seductive offers. Once we have made the decision to go ahead with an offer, we no longer voice any objections. Our fate is sealed.

In order to repulse the greed factor, we have to keep in mind that most of these offers are "too good to be true." How many people do you personally know who have won a new car or a free trip, or who are earning over $100,000 annually? We must separate the myth from the everyday reality.

Remember these "myths":

•You can earn a six figure income your first year in this business.

•If you don't sign up now, this opportunity won't be available later.

•You are the only person who we are talking to about this offer.

•You can start making a profit the first day you open your business.

•You can work only a few hours a week and make big dollars in this business.

•You won't have to spend more than your initial investment to make this business successful.

•The product will sell itself.

•Nothing to It•

"The Ease Factor" is the second clue to helping us understand why we make a particular choice. Americans strive for a "life of ease." Beware of anyone telling you how easy it is. Whether it's making money, selling the product, redeeming the prize, or taking the dream vacation, most things of value take time and effort to achieve. You also may be told that no special training, aptitude, or experience is necessary. Nothing is that easy as hard work is required to be successful.

•Beat the Clock•

The **"Time Factor"** is the third clue. Americans have learned the pleasures of instant gratification. We tend to be impatient and want to make things happen right now.

Consider the source when you are told it will not take long to start earning money or profits. Remember, any new business venture takes time to develop, be successful, and be profitable.

•What's Up Doc?•

You can't be too skeptical in today's world. If something has grabbed your attention, ask yourself the following questions:

•Am I reacting or responding to advertising or sales hype?

•Is this something I am acquainted with or have I decided on this new venture without getting all the necessary information?

•What part do the "Greed Factor," "Ease Factor," or "Time Factor" play in my decision?

The promise that you can become rich quickly and easily appeals to almost everyone. If you can recognize the factors that the salesperson is appealing to, then you will be able to assess the situation and make a proper decision.

Next: Advertising Used In Scams

12

Advertising Used In Scams

> *"Of money, wit, and virtue,*
> *believe one-fourth of what you hear."*
> Proverb

•The Bold and the Beautiful•

Advertising aims at catching the eye and stimulating an emotional response. Just as important as the product is the packaging appeal. In many cases, it is the advertising we read or see that grabs our attention. Ads trigger our interest and make us want to have what we see or read. In our busy lives, we are constantly bombarded by ads that are found on radio, television, magazines, newspapers, signs, etc.

Often advertisements are not what they profess to be. The Federal Trade Commission has rules regarding advertising but cannot check or verify all the millions of ads as to their content or quality. There are many reputable companies that use advertising correctly but also others that don't hesitate to abuse the system.

Do you know these facts about the power of advertising?

✓America uses 57% of the world's advertising while it only

includes 6% of the world's population.

✓ It is estimated that manufacturers spend more than $45 billion a year on advertising and more than $60 billion a year on various types of product promotions such as coupons, rebates, premiums, free samples, etc.

✓ In the U.S., there are a total of 1,220 television stations, 9,871 radio stations, 482 newspapers, and 11,328 newspapers.

✓ Every year, the average American watches 1,550 hours of TV, listens to 1,160 hours of radio, and reads 180 hours of newspapers and 110 hours of magazines.

✓ The average person will watch more than 100 TV ads a day (watching 30 hours of TV a week and approximately 37,822 commercials per year) and are likely to hear or see another 100 to 300 ads per day from radio, newspapers, magazines, and signs.[11]

•The Postman Rings Twice•

It is up to us, the consumers, to carefully scrutinize and critique the advertising we see. We respond differently to various types of advertisements depending on what appeals to us.

We must concern ourselves with three different types of advertising:

1) The first type is advertising that arrives in the mail. This would include unsolicited mail such as a sweepstakes, mail order ads, investment ads, etc.

2) The second type would be solicited information that you might request from a company about a particular offer. This could include a company's financial statement, brochure, or written information on a business opportunity or prize giveaway.

[11]Pratkanis, Anthony and Aranson, Elliot, Age of Propaganda, W. H. Feldman, New York, NY, 3-4.

3) The third type of advertising would be found in the classified ads and display ads found in newspapers and magazines.

I have provided the following examples of advertisements to alert you to the many phrases that might make an ad turn out to be an fraudulent offer.

Here is an example of an unsolicited postcard ad:

You are a grand prize winner! You have won one of three fantastic prizes listed below. You have only 24 hours to call and redeem your prize. If you do not call quickly, your prize will be given to someone else. Call 1-900-555-5555 now to find out what prize you have won!		
A giant screen projection TV	A luxury automobile	A dream vacation to Hawaii
There is no obligation to purchase anything. Don't miss out, call 1-900-555-5555 to receive your prize!		

These are similar examples of some solicited advertising that was sent by a company regarding its business opportunity:

Thanks for calling us and listening to our presentation on our very successful business opportunity. We have a new marketing breakthrough in a very popular industry. We are a major distributing company. We work on a national basis with many companies, corporations, and retailers. We are now establishing a network of distributors and salespeople who will represent our company locally.

We need distributors. As a distributor, you may hire, train and manage salespeople. A distributor should be able to earn more than $100,000 a year which includes your first year in business. You can work either full time or part time.

Your investment includes complete inventory and training information.

This opportunity is second to no others. There are two ways to market our hot new product. First is to use our full-color retail displays. The second method (most profitable) is by using our exciting new sales program with businesses.

This fabulous business opportunity makes you money two ways. First, you sell our product in large volume numbers. There is great customer demand for our product. Second, there is a constant need for reorders, too. You not only make money on the sale but for months or years afterwards. **Now doesn't this sound like the one of the best business opportunites you have ever heard of? (Now be honest!)** Information on owning a protected territory is also available. Call 1-800-555-5555 for more information.

* * * * * * * * *

Join us and be a part of America's hottest new business opportunity. New states and areas are just opening up. This exciting new business opportunity with our company offers you financial freedom and a whole new way to live. You can join people all over America who are cashing in. You are going to discover one of the finest businesses in our country today. And that's a guarantee. Our distributors make money, live as they please, and just as important, they have fun and enjoy the business. There isn't any other business that I know of that offers the rewards that our company does. Our distributors are reaching goals (both financial and personal) that they never thought were possible. The figures and projections for this business are outstanding even during economic slumps. **Isn't this business a winner? You can bet your life!**

* * * * * * * * *

The Reasons Why Our
Distributors Are So Successful

•A "hot" new product on the market;

•A service business the customer needs;

•Constant reorders;

•Great profits;

•Outstanding commissions plus residuals;

•Immediate income;

•New areas and states available;

•You are your own boss;

•Low or no overhead;

•Minimum inventory required;

•Huge tax advantages;

•Incredible returns on your investment;

•No royalties;

•Flexible hours;

•Full- or part-time;

•Light work;

•Comprehensive training manual;

•Sales management guides;

•Full-color retail displays available;

•100% corporate backup;

•Work out of your home;

•Free salesperson placement program;

•Big overrides with each redemption;

•Full corporate training;

•Ongoing repeat business;

•Full collateral backup;

•Protected territories available (call for details).

* * * * * * * * *

Similar advertisements to the next two were run in a Denver newspaper by a company named Master Industries which was promoting a business opportunity. This turned out to be a scam. The first ad appeared in 1971 and the second in 1973. These types of ads could still be effectively used today.

WE NEED MANAGEMENT PEOPLE
WHO CAN SEE AN OPPORTUNITY,
GRAB IT, AND RUN WITH IT!

Authentic opportunities do not come by too often in a man or woman's life. Usually they are ignored or put off until it's too late. A four years young international marketing corporation headquartered in Denver has already made its mark in marketing history with phenomenal growth already having over 600 associates. It is a leader in a dynamic new field which has little competition and a fantastic future. We are seeking men and women of management calibre with enough guts, determination, and savvy to carve out a market that is literally crying for our service, managers who don't have to have their hands held, who know they are not being paid their real worth. If you want to be challenged to the limits of your abilities, and paid very well, contact Ms. Jones at 333-3333.

* * * * * * * * *

Have You Ever Wondered
Why Men/Women Earning
$100,000 a Year
Become Distributors for Our
Products? Or Why Some of:

Our distributors drive luxury automobiles;
Our distributors fly their own airplanes;

Our distributors travel abroad every year;
Our distributors own their own office buildings;
Our distributors are authors in demand as public speakers;
Our distributors are leaders in religious and civic affairs;
If you have ever wondered what the other side (the true side)
of this great success story is, you owe it to yourself to find
out! Our opportunity might be just what you've been
looking for! Write or call us for our free information.

* * * * * * * * *

•Ring My Chimes•

Included below are what I feel could fit the category of
questionable phrases or "jingles" used in advertising. I call
these ads "come-on ads" because they trigger our emotions and
make us want "to take action."

**The following phrases could represent red flags when
you see them:**
•Do you want to be rich and famous;
•Become a Fat Cat;
•Six-figure income;
•Earn $100,000 or earn $10,000 a month;
•Financial freedom;
•No selling necessary;
•Ground floor opportunity;
•Money maker or money machine;
•Easy money;
•Incredible profits;
•500% profit;
•Make over $____ an hour or $____ per day;
•Earn ____% on your money guaranteed;
•No risk investment;

•Incredible overrides or residuals;
•Complete, full, or 100% corporate training, support, or backup;
•Your cost as little as $____;
•Ongoing repeat business;
•Low overhead or no overhead;
•If you want to make a lot of money or get rich, call us now;
•Unlimited earnings;
•No inventory needed;
•You can easily become a millionaire;
•I started my own business for only $____;
•Marketing breakthrough;
•Products at below wholesale prices;
•No investment required; Start without any capital;
•How to become wealthy or grow rich;
•How to make a financial killing;
•Turn your spare hours into big income;
•Deal direct, no middleman, keep all profits;
•Special introductory offer or limited time offer;
•Hurry or you will miss out;
•Be financially independent;
•The safest opportunity of the '90s;
•Chance of a lifetime;
•Too good to pass up;
•Protected territories available;
•How to make big money at home;
•I guarantee you to make $____ or I'll double your money back
    or I'll send you an extra $____ back;
•Income day one or first day profits;
•You have won one of three fantastic gifts;
•To receive your free prize, hurry and call 1-900-;
•If you are not completely satisfied with my offer after 3 years,
    I will gladly refund your money.

                    *   *   *   *   *   *   *   *

The following are examples of personal endorsements or testimonials which further convince the prospect of the crediblility of a particular company:

"We just had to let you know that we are averaging between $6,000 and $9,000 per month in our business checking account. We absolutely love the business." *Allegheny Promotions*
* * * * * * * * *

"Jamie and I have been working full time at the business using all the information and resources contained in your sales training and business manual. The information is absolutely invaluable. We couldn't have been successful without it." *J and D Enterprises*
* * * * * * * * *

"You and your entire staff have been just wonderful answering our tough questions. We have signed up two major accounts which should help us attain a goal of $300,000 in earnings by year's end." *Mercury and Associates*
* * * * * * * * *

"It is really remarkable. I have made more money in the last three months than I made all of last year. Becoming a distributor with your company was the best decision I have ever made in my life." *Albert D. Johnson*
* * * * * * * * *

•Cool Hand Luke•

Don't let your emotions get carried away by the advertisements you see. **Keep your cool. Decide carefully whether you want to pick up the phone and call on an ad.**

Next: The Law

13

The Law

fraud n. "deceit, trickery, an intentional attempt to deprive you of money, property, or a lawful right, breach of confidence perpetrated for profit" (Random House Dictionary of the English Language 1987, 2nd Edition, Unabridged, Random House, New York, NY).

•The Trickster•

Fraud has become a way of life in our society. History is loaded with fraudulent people, businesses, and governments. Many states are passing legislation with stiffer penalties. New laws are taking away many of the con man's escape loopholes. The draw of huge sums of money continues to entice new individuals into this fraudulent billion dollar industry.

There are a number of governmental regulatory agencies, both locally and nationally, that investigate and prosecute these tricksters of deceit. Unfortunately, these agencies have neither the manpower nor the funding to handle the increasing caseload of complaints. Most of these agencies will not pursue an individual case or claim against an unethical company. It takes a large number of complaints for them to bring an action against a specific company. **However, it is imperative that you file a complaint about these unethical activities.** This complaint places the name of the offending company on record and could be instrumental in helping you or others at a later date.

It can be very frustrating when an individual calls one of these agencies or companies to inquire about possible complaints or any investigations regarding a specific company. Generally, he is told that all information is confidential and not available to the public. This makes it seem as if these agencies are working against the consumer rather than helping to protect him/her. The consumer's only choice is to file a complaint with the proper agency and wait to see if any action is taken against the unethical company. If any action is pursued against an offending company, the outcome of this action is usually seen in the newspaper or on the television news rather than by direct notification of the person or persons who filed the complaints.

•Small Potatoes•

Now, there seems to be much more cooperation among law enforcement agencies in pursuing illegal activities. Recently, a group in Denver called "TAG" banded together to put a fraudulent telemarketing operation out of business. The FBI, the IRS, the U.S. Post Office, the Colorado Attorney General, and the Denver District Attorney all worked in cooperation to convict the offenders. Also, the US Attorney General's "Boiler Room Task Force" has obtained several hundred convictions during the last few years.

Lighter sentences are often imposed on the convicted swindlers. It is very difficult to have these offenses considered with the same seriousness as more violent crimes such as murder, assault, rape, burglary, and drug dealing. Fraud is considered "small potatoes" or "petty fraud" when compared with these more violent crimes.

A telemarketing company placed under investigation or closed up quickly opens up down the street using a new name and a slightly different premise or product. The ease and relatively inexpensive mode of operation contributes to the speed of implementing an old company into an entirely new one.

As salespeople graduate and move on to open their own illegal operations, the telemarketing business continues to flourish. Telemarketing fraud continues to proliferate on a nationwide basis. The success of these companies lies in their ability to avoid detection or prosecution. The majority of offenders are not afraid of getting caught. They know fraud is difficult to prove in the courts. By locating their businesses in different states from where they conduct their business, these companies remain relatively free from any legal action.

•Getting It Right•

What needs to be done to protect the general public from these dishonest companies?

First, make sure you file a complaint if you think you might be involved in a scam.

Second, write or talk to your Senators and Representatives about the problem of consumer being ripped off. When our political representatives see and hear enough people demanding action, then the laws will change.

We, the consumers, need to promote the passage of new federal legislation. One of the most important pieces of legislation, if passed as a law, would give each citizen the right to sue a company located out of state and to make that company defend itself in the citizen's own local federal court. These companies would then be forced to spend their money and time defending themselves on our territory.

Next: S-C-A-M: The Meaning

PART THREE
Fighting
Back

14
S-C-A-M: The Meaning

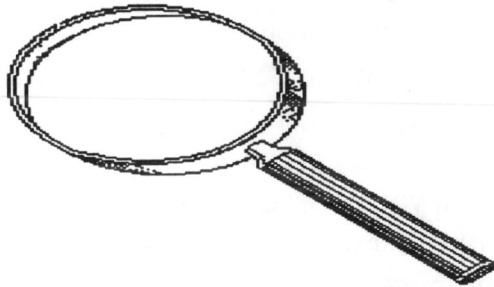

•Sherlock Holmes•

As a tool, I have assigned each letter in the word **"scam"** to have a specific job. Using these methods I describe will enable you to sift out the good opportunities from the bad.

S=Skeptical

C=Collect

A=Analyze

M=Motive

S=Skeptical:

•Could it Be True?•

This word speaks for itself. Be skeptical and suspicious of any unsolicited telephone calls, mail, or advertisements you receive with information on a product, service, business opportunity, free prize or gift, etc.

C=Collect:

•Let the Record Speak for Itself•

This word refers to the collection process. Keep a detailed journal or notebook with all the records of telephone conversations and correspondence you have had with the prospective company regarding its offer. Be very detailed as to the dates and times of all telephone calls and what was said or discussed. A folder is also an ideal way of organizing all written information and brochures that you have received from the company. Then you will be able to go back and carefully analyze all the information you have gathered. The information you collect could be critical should you choose to bring legal action or file a complaint with a governmental agency.

Check out the opportunity as thoroughly as possible by calling the list of agencies and businesses I mention in the next chapter. These agencies or businesses could provide you with additional information regarding the company, its product, and its giveaway.

Ask the salesperson for several business references and any additional references of people who are presently selling or using the product (preferably in your state). **If the company is legitimate, references will not be a problem.** Fabrications may be a part of some references so caution is always advised. Do not make your decision solely on what these references tell you.

•Playing the Devil's Advocate•

Remember when you ask the questions, you are in a position of power. Here is a list of questions you can use to ask the salesperson:

•How did you get my name?

•Can you give me several references on your company and its principals?

•How long has your company been in business?

•Will you send me a brochure or other written information on your company and its product?

•Would you be willing to explain your proposal to my attorney, accountant, or banker?

•How much of my investment is used toward commissions and fees?

•What governmental and regulatory agencies supervise your business activity?

•Will you please send me a copy of your contract so I can have my attorney look it over?

•If you are going to hold my money, where will you keep it?

•Do you provide regular statements about my investment? How often? What kind?

•Do you have a money back guarantee? Will you send me a copy of it?

•Are there any lawsuits pending against your company?

When you obtain the names and phone numbers of people who have used the product, have received the prize, or have taken the free trip, make sure you talk to each one of these individuals. Call other companies or people in your local area who might be possible users or buyers of the product in order to find out if they have ever heard of the company and its product or offer.

Let this list of questions lead you to making the right decision:

•Would a company or a consumer be interested in such a product?

•Is there any competition for the product?

•Do you know of any other salespeople selling your identical product or a similar product?

•What is the market for the product?

•Does the product or prize really have the value advertised?

•Could I sell the product or prize at my cost and recoup my investment?

Other questions you could ask a distributor or seller of the product:

•Do you know anything negative or have you heard any complaints about this company, its offer, or its product?

•Are you aware of any lawsuits against this company?

•What do you not like about this company?

•How does the company treat you?

•How good is the company's training and service?

•How easy or difficult is this business?

•How long did it take you to start making money?

•How many hours do you work a week?

•Would you please tell me how much money you made your first year? Was that net or gross income?

•Will the company give me my investment back if I find I cannot sell the product?

•What realistic income can I expect to earn my first year?

•Would you invest again with this same company?

•Would you suggest I invest in this opportunity?

Some important reminders:
1) Find out if a payment is required before services are rendered.
2) Check with your local consumer protection agency, your state attorney general's office, and your district attorney's office to see if any complaints have been filed against this company.
3) Always read the contract carefully before signing. Don't hesitate to ask questions or seek legal advice.
4) Is the salesperson making claims that aren't included in writing? Always get all representations in writing so there are no misunderstandings later.

A=Analyze:
•Taking Charge•

Make sure you carefully evaluate all your notes and information. It is important you arrive at a correct decision based on what you know as hard facts rather than assumptions. To help with your decision making, divide a piece of paper down the middle and make a list of all the positives and negatives about this offer.

Do not feel pressured. Time is your ally, not your foe. Use it to your best advantage. The more time you take to think about an offer, the more the odds improve in your favor that you will make a correct decision. Take as long as you need to study all the information you have collected. Listen to what you have learned. Do not go against what you know to be true.

M=Motive:
•Was It Your Head or Your Heart?•

This is very important in evaluating your own motives or your reasons for reaching a particular decision.

Ask yourself the following questions:

•Are you looking for a way to make money quickly?

•How much financial pressure are you feeling?

•Why are you looking at this type of opportunity or offer?

•What caught your interest about this opportunity or offer?

•Why do you need this opportunity or offer so much?

•Is your spouse or family supportive of this opportunity?

•Are you sure you can sell or use the product?

•How much do you really know about this business or offer?

•Have you researched this type of business or offer?

•Does the company really care about you?

•Are you willing to invest more money in order to get this venture started?

•Do you have enough money saved or extra income to cover your living expenses until your business is generating usable income?

•Here Comes the Judge•

Consider your motives carefully. These motives should tell you whether your reasons are good enough for reaching a specific decision.

The following page includes an easy to use evaluation form for an offer or opportunity. (This form may also be found as an easy-to-use copy page in the back of the book.)

Next: Who to Call for Help?

✔An Evaluation of an Offer✔

✔This checklist is strictly a guide to use to help you arrive at a correct decision.

✔Name of company:_____

✔The address:_____

✔City, state, zip code:_____

✔Phone no:_____

✔Date of 1st call: _____

✔Name of person:_____

✔Who called whom? _____

✔What did you first talk about?_____
_____

✔How did you hear about the offer?_____
_____

✔How many years has the company been in business?___

✔How good is this offer? _____

✔Are you requesting more information to be mailed to you?
_____What was the company's attitude?_____
_____

✔Will the company provide you with references? (preferrably in your state) _____
names and phone numbers:_____
_____

✔Are you being pressured to sign up or pay with a credit card?_____

✔Is there any obligation to purchase anything in order to receive the offer? _____

✔How much do you know about this kind of offer or business?_____ Have you read the fine print?____

✔Are you being promised things that are "too good to be true?"_____ How risky is this offer? _____

✔Make sure you always get other opinions on this offer from friends, business associates, or an attorney.

15

Who to Call for Help?

•Who Can I Turn To?•

In this chapter, you will find a list of agencies and companies, both private and governmental, to contact if you come in contact with a scam. You will also find a wealth of educational information available to the public. (Most of this information is free.)

Awareness is the first step in prevention. It is very important that you report your suspicions or your evidence to as many agencies as possible. Your call may trigger an investigation and could result in criminal charges being filed against the fraudulent company. As each complaint is logged and dated with an agency, a stronger and stronger case is built.

Contacting the radio and television media can also bring powerful results. Flooding the airwaves with an alarm can bring a quicker resolution to your problem and alerts the general public to the profile of the scam-in-action.

Remember, silence is what contributes to a scam's success. **Breaking the silence by reporting the scam not only helps you, but also benefits many other consumers as well.**

Whether making phone calls or writing letters, you will be surprised how much better you feel when you have taken positive steps against these swindlers. So don't procrastinate. Pick up your pen and start writing or grab the phone and call now. **You can make a difference!**

If you think you are involved in a fraudulent situation, here is a list of suggestions on who you might call to file a complaint or to get information:
1) Call the National Fraud Information Center at 1-800-876-7060.
2) Call your local District Attorney.
3) Call your State Attorney General's Office.
4) Call any other agencies or companies listed in this chapter which could help you or which would investigate your specific kind of fraud.
5) Call your local media (newspapers, radio and television stations for their consumer advocate).

The following is a list of possible companies and agencies from which to gather educational information and/or to pursue your complaints:

Local Agencies and Companies

•District Attorney's Office•
The local District Attorney's Office investigates fraud cases and provides consumer complaint lines as well as educational

information. Generally, it will mail you free information regarding telemarketing and other frauds. It is located in your local phone book under your city or county government section listing for District Attorney.

•Local Radio Stations, Television Stations, and Newspapers•

Many radio and television stations have "Consumer Awareness Shows" and "Consumer Affairs Specialists" who would like to hear your story. If the fraud was committed locally, it could be an excellent forum for your story and also a possible catalyst to starting an investigation and eventually getting your money returned. Contact your local stations. Also do not hesitate to contact your local newspaper.

•State Attorney General's Office•

This agency accepts complaints, investigates and prosecutes frauds. It is generally located in your local telephone book if you live in your state capitol and is usually found in the state government section under the State Attorney General's Office. You also may obtain the number by calling long-distance information for the state government listings in your capitol city, 1-area code-555-1212.

•State/Local Consumer Affairs or Fraud Department•

Most states have a Consumer Fraud Division or Consumer Protection Unit. This state or local agency generally takes complaints and investigates telemarketing fraud. (It may be listed under your State Attorney General's office or local District Attorney's office.) Call local information or 1-area code-555-1212 to find the number.

•State Division of Securities•

This state agency helps regulate and investigate state securities dealers and investments. Call local information or 1-area code-555-1212 to find the phone number for your State's Division of Securities.

•U.S. Postal Service (local)•

The U.S. Postal Service investigates complaints and prosecutes fraudulent businesses that use the mails to sell or advertise their product. Mail fraud may also include telemarketing and newspaper advertising because money is sometimes sent through the mail in response to these ads. For more information on frauds, contact your local Postmaster or call on the new "Postal Answer Line" (in most cities listed in your telephone book under U.S. Government, Postal Service).

•Victim Assistance Agencies•

These agencies help advise people who have been taken advantage of by frauds, scams, and other crimes. They can be found in many larger cities in the phone book under listings such as Victim Assistance, Victim Services Center, or Victim Outreach Information.

National Agencies and Companies

•American Association of Retired Persons (AARP)•

AARP has an excellent educational program. It is called "What Can You Do About Crime?" and includes 13 videotape programs available to the public for loan or purchase. Also available is the book, "Investor Alert." Send for your free catalog of titles (D13655) to AARP Fulfillment (EE0114),

1909 K St. N.W., Washington, DC 20049. Allow 6 to 8 weeks for delivery. You can get further information by calling toll free at 1-800-424-3410.

•American Society of Travel Agents•

You may receive a free pamphlet entitled "Avoiding Travel Problems" by writing the American Society of Travel Agents, Consumer Affairs, P.O. Box 23992, Washington, DC 20026-3992.

•Better Business Bureau (BBB)•

You can call this company about possible scams, but it has no powers to investigate or prosecute. The BBB has offices in many cities all over the country. It provides educational materials on many kinds of frauds, and could be helpful when you are personally investigating a company. The BBB may be able to provide you with a written report on the company you are investigating as well as tell you if there are any complaints against this company. You must call the BBB in the city and state where the company is located. For the telephone number of the BBB in your city or state, look in your local telephone book or call 1-703-276-0100. Most BBB offices have a "Tele-Tips" phone line that you can call and listen to educational, taped information about various subjects including different types of telemarketing frauds. As another service, the BBB offers a **Philanthropic Advisory Bureau** which rates various charitable and non-profit organizations. To reach this bureau, also call 1-703-276-0100.

•Business Radio Network•

This is an excellent way for you to air your information about a scam. This network has a talk-radio program called "Scams across America" which is heard weekly on approximately 50 stations nationwide. Call Richard Cooper with your information at 1-719-528-7040, fax number 1-719-528-5170, or write c/o BRN, 888 Garden of the Gods Rd., Colorado Springs, CO 80907.

•Central Phone Number for Congress•

This is an excellent avenue to talk to your Congressmens' or Senators' office in Washington and voice your opinions and complaints. You can call the central number for Congress in Washington at 1-202-224-3121 and you will be connected with your representatives' office.

If you would like to receive any governmental committee's free report or the latest report by the Committee on Government Operations on Telemarketing Fraud titled "The scourge of telemarketing fraud: What can be done against it?", call 1-202-225-3456 and ask for report #102-421, December 91.

•Commodity Futures Trading Commission•

This commission regulates and investigates commodity trading. For information, write the Commodity Futures Trading Commission, 2033 K St., N.W., Washington, DC 20581 or call 1-202-254-6387. For complaints, write the CFTC, 2000 L St., NW, Rm. 620, Washington, DC 20581 or call 1-202-254-3067.

•Consumer Health Information Research Institute (CHIRI)•

This institute offers health information for the consumer. It is especially helpful in making sure you arrive at the correct health decision and also has educational brochures available to the public. The director is John Renner, M.D., who is an authority on "quackery." Call with your questions toll free at 1-800-821-6671 or write Dr. Renner in care of CHIRI, 3521 Broadway, Kansas City, MO 64111.

•Direct Marketing Association•

You can write this company requesting that you want to stop receiving junk mail. However, mail that is addressed to "occupant" can't be stopped. Send your request (include as many variations of your name, address, or initials as you can think of) to the Mail Preference Service, c/o Direct Marketing Association, P.O. Box 9008, Farmingdale, NY 11735. It could take as long as four to six months to see some action.

•Dun and Bradstreet•

This company offers business information on millions of U.S. businesses. D&B disseminates information about a business' operations and its principals, including company history, management experience, financial condition, payments to vendors, corporate charter details, banking information and public filings (suits, liens, judgements, bankruptcies and UCCs). Businesses may subscribe to the service on an annual basis or order individual reports at a cost of $60 through D&B Express Services. For more information or to order a report, call toll free 1-800-TRY1DNB, extension 1199 (1-800-879-1362). D&B has offices in most major cities.

•Environmental Protection Agency•

This governmental agency is able to answer your environmental questions regarding radon and water quality. It will direct the consumer to certified water testing labs or state water quality agencies. You may call their information number at 1-202-260-2090 for information on the many available toll-free 800 number "Hotlines." For the "safe drinking water hotline" call 1-800-426-4791 or for the "Radon Hotline" call 1-800-767-7236. If you live in Washington, DC, call 382-5533. Or you can write the EPA, 401 M St. S.W., Washington, DC 20460.

•Federal Trade Commission•

This agency investigates and prosecutes advertising and investment frauds. It does not pursue individual actions or claims, but your complaints may be very helpful in developing a particular case against a company. Please send any complaints to the Bureau of Consumer Protection, c/o Federal Trade Commission, 6th and Pennsylvania Ave., Washington, D. 20580. To get information or receive any of their 75 different free educational pamphlets (ex: "900 number Scams," "Most Prevalent Scams," etc.), write the Public Reference Room c/o FTC at the above address or call 1-202-326-2222.

•Food and Drug Administration•

This U. S. agency provides information about products that are mislabled, misrepresented, or harmful. For information, write the FDA, c/o Consumer Affairs and Information, 5600 Fishers Lane, HFC-10, Rockville, MD 20857 or call toll free at 1-800-858-3760.

•Insurance Rating Services•

If you are buying an insurance policy or an annuity, it is important to check the company's safety ratings (financial stability). There are five rating services. 1) A.M. Best has a customer service department at 1-908-439-2200 (Best rates 3,800 insurers, and there is a fee for its ratings; 2) Standard and Poor's offers free ratings of 525 companies at 1-212-208-1527; 3) Moody provides free ratings of 264 companies at 1-212-553-0377; 4) Duff and Phelps has free ratings of 115 companies at 1-312-368-3157; 5) Weiss Research charges a fee at 1-800-289-9222.

Always ask for an explanation of each company's insurance ratings and ask if there are any charges to you. Make your own choice based on the following criteria:1) The company should be rated A-double-plus or A-plus by A. M. Best; 2) be one of the top two or three listings from one of the other major raters; 3) and should not be rated below the fourth category by any of the major raters. **Do your homework.**

•Medicare or Medicaid Hotline•

Make sure you call regarding any suspicious activity or suspected fraud with Medicare or Medicaid to the government's toll-free "Fraud Hotline" at 1-800-368-5779.

•National Association of Securities Dealers•

The NASD is a private company that regulates and investigates the Nasdaq (national over the counter stock market). This company works very closely with the SEC. It can tell you if a particular dealer or company is licensed, if the proper papers have been filed, and if a prospectus is available. To get the work and disciplinary history of a broker, call 1-800-289-9999. All complaints must be in writing and mailed to the district office servicing your area. There are 14 district offices. For more information call 1-202-728-8000 or your local district office.

•National Center for Financial Education•

This non-profit organization offers a 41 page guide to help consumers repair and improve their credit. To get a copy of the "Do-It-Yourself Credit and Improvement Guide," send $10 to the NCFE, P.O. Box 34070, San Diego, CA 92163-4070.

•National Charities Information Bureau•

Send for a free copy of the "Wise Giving Guide" to the National Charities Information Bureau, 19 Union Square West, 6th floor, New York, NY 10003 or call for information at 1-212-929-6300.

•National Committee for Responsible Philanthropy•

This private organization monitors and writes reports on foundations and charities. You can order reports at a cost of $15 to $25. For more information, write to the National Committee for Responsible Philanthropy, 2001 S St. N.W., Suite 620, Washington, DC 20009 or call 1-202-387-9177.

•National Consumers League•

The National Consumers League has a 1-800-fraud hotline called the **"National Fraud Information Center."** The toll-free fraud hotline number is **1-800-876-7060.** This non-profit organization also has a sub agency called the **"Alliance Against Fraud in Telemarketing."** It is composed of federal, state, trade union, industrial, and consumer groups. Mail them your complaint, and it will be forwarded to the appropriate agency that investigates and prosecutes that particular type of fraud. Send your complaints to the Alliance Against Fraud in Telemarketing, c/o National Consumers League, 815 15th St. N. W., Suite 516, Washington, DC 20005. It also offers a 200 page "Consumer Protection Handbook" ($45).To receive information, free brochures, and educational material on telemarketing frauds, you may write to the above address or call 1-202-639-8140.

•National Council Against Health Fraud•

If you want to start legal action against a so called "quack," this is the organization to call. You will be referred to an experienced attorney who handles cases of health fraud. The Council offers a list of possible expert witnesses and may also be able to provide facts about defense witnesses. Also available is a list of possible fraudulent and dangerous health treatments. For information and questions, contact Michael Botts, c/o National Council Against Health Fraud, P.O. Box 333008,

Kansas City, MO 64114 or call 1-816-444-8615.

•National Fraud Information Center•

If you think you might have information about a fraud or a scam, make sure you call this toll-free fraud hotline, **1-800-876-7060.** You can speak to a counselor or be referred to the proper agency. Or you can access a computer bulletin board **(National Fraud Information Center Electronic Gateway)** by modem using IBM-compatible PCs at **1-202-347-3189.** You can talk to "experts" and gather information on the latest scams. The National Consumers League's "Consumer Protection Handbook" is also on line for your use.

•National Futures Association•

This is a self-regulatory organization for all brokerage firms and registered individuals selling commodity futures such as soy beans, sugar, foreign currencies, petroleum, gold, silver, platinum, etc. When reporting a fraud, call toll free at 1-800-621-3570 (in Illinois, 1-800-572-9400) or write National Futures Association, 200 W. Madison St., Suite 1600, Chicago, IL 60606-3447.

•National Insurance Crime Bureau•

This bureau was established in an effort by insurers to eliminate fraudulent and inflated insurance claims. This company also takes calls about any insurance crimes such as auto thefts, insurance frauds, etc. You may call a toll free consumer educational and complaint hotline. The toll free phone number is 1-800-835-6422 (TEL-NICB). Some states have implemented their own insurance fraud hotlines.

•National Insurance Information Institute•

This company answers your general insurance questions and will also send you educational brochures on all kinds of insurance. The toll-free number is 1-800-221-4954.

•North American Securities Administrators Association•

This is a national regulatory organization composed of state securities agencies. It regulates investments and the companies that sell them. Call 1-202-737-0900 for the address and phone number of your own state's securities agency or call your state government's information number. Also call to receive a list of free brochures and information on telemarketing fraud or write the NASAA at 555 New Jersey Ave., N.W., Suite 750, Washington, DC 20001.

•Philanthropic Advisory Service (part of the BBB)•

Before making a decision regarding any donation to a non-profit or charitable organization, send for the report called "Update on Charitable Organizations." You need to include $1.00 plus a self-addressed, stamped return envelope and mail it to: Philanthropic Advisory Service, 4200 Wilson Blvd., Arlington, VA 22203 or for more information call 1-703-276-0100.

•Private Investigative Services•

If you are considering a large investment opportunity, you may want to use a private investigation service. It could be worth it for you to spend some extra money to thoroughly check out the professional background on any franchise or business opportunity as well as their employees. Look in the Yellow Pages under "Investigators" or you could call the Pinkerton Investigative Services toll free at 1-800-232-7465 for more information and ask for a free copy of their brochure entitled "Employers' Guide to Investigative Services."

•Securities and Exchange Commission (SEC)•

This federal agency regulates and investigates the securities industry including public companies, investment brokers, and transfer agents. The SEC has regional offices located in New York, Boston, Philadelphia, Washington D.C., Chicago, Atlanta, Denver, Ft. Worth, Los Angeles, and Seattle. You need to call the office in the regional city that you think might handle the complaint. Each SEC office has an information and complaint phone line. The long-distance information number is 1-area code-555-1212. Ask for the Security and Exchange Commission under U.S. government listings. For the federal records of complaints, write the SEC Freedom of Information Branch, 450 Fifth St., N.W., Mail Stop 2-6, Washington, DC 20549.

•Television Networks (ABC, CBS, NBC, CNN)•

All of these major television networks have consumer specialists or reporters who are interested in all types of frauds and scams. More and more stories are being aired about all kinds of frauds. Television can provide dramatic results. Do not hesitate to call these networks or your local television or radio stations in order to tell your story.
ABC 1-212-456-7777;   CBS 1-212-975-4321;
NBC 1-212-664-4444;   CNN 1-404-827-1500;

•U.S. Postal Service•

This agency has now implemented a new "postal answer line" in most major cities. This phone line has extensions with information on various types of frauds. Check with your local post office or for more information, write the Chief Postal

Inspector, US Post Office Department, Washington, DC 20262.
(More information on the US Postal Service may be found
under local agencies, page 128.)

Next: Five Easy Rules for Avoiding Scams

16

Five Easy Rules for Avoiding Scams

•Scambusters•

Following these rules consistently will save you financial losses and emotional heartaches. Keep this list of rules by your phone, on your refrigerator, or anywhere else that is handy for reference. Read these rules on a regular basis until you have memorized them.

Rule #1: **Do not get involved if your common sense tells you it is "too good to be true."** Most scams will fit in the category of being "too good to be true."

Rule #2: **Do not purchase or invest any money with a person you do not know personally, whether over the phone, in person, or by mail.**

If it is the salesperson who first initiates the call, it is best to end the call. If you initiate the call yourself, make sure you know who you are talking to about an offer. In most cases, following this rule will save you money and frustration. Use good sense. Ask yourself, why would I consider investing or purchasing something over the phone from a stranger?

Here are two simple rebuttals you can use to stop telemarketing solicitations:
1) "Sorry, but I do not conduct business over the phone with people I do not know."
2) "Sorry, but I do not accept any phone solicitations."

<u>Rule #3:</u> **Do not do business with a company located out of state.**
    It is better to be on the side of safety. If possible, deal with companies inside your state. Therefore, you avoid the headaches and problems of legal recourse with a company located out of state.

<u>Rule #4:</u> **Do not invest unless you can afford to lose your investment.**

<u>Rule #5:</u> **Do not give your personal credit card numbers or other account numbers to a stranger by telephone or by mail.** (This also includes long-distance phone card numbers, social security numbers, checking account numbers, insurance policy information or account numbers, etc.) **Watch out as someone could be looking over your shoulder!**

*The exceptions to rules 2, 3, and 5 would occur only if you feel sure you can trust the company or person with whom you are conducting business.

Utilizing these rules in combination with "The Factors" in Chapter 11, "Advertising Used in Scams" in Chapter 12, and "S-C-A-M: The Meaning" in Chapter 14, furnishes you with all the practical information you should need to make sure you will resist even the most inviting scams.

"Five Easy Rules for Avoiding Scams" may also be found in the appendix as a easy-to-use copy page.

Next: Tips for Senior Citizens

PART FOUR
Senior Citizen
Alert

17

Tips For Senior Citizens

> *"Education is no guarantee of wisdom,*
> *but it sure increases the likelihood."*
> Unknown

•For the Young at Heart•

One of the most popular groups of people attracting the scam artist is the senior citizen. According to the American Association of Retired Persons (AARP), senior citizens represent slightly more than 12.5% of the overall U.S. population, or approximately 31 million people. Studies show that currently the senior citizen remains a prime prospect for a scam. Having more money in reserve, often a home clear of debt, and extra assets from retirement plans, savings accounts, and social security as well as other investments, the senior citizen is in an enviable position.

These older Americans came from an era where honesty was very important. A handshake and eye-to-eye contact meant more and was honored like a contract. A person's word was especially significant. People trusted each other much more than they do today.

Here are some statistics on why senior citizens are targeted:

☑ In 1983, the total income of those over 65 years of age was $263 billion.[12]

☑ It has been estimated that those over the age of 50 control over half of the discretionary income and own more than 77 percent of the assets in the U.S.

☑ Households that are headed by a person 50 years of age or older have over $950 billion in annual income and a net worth of $7 trillion.[13]

☑ Half the population of the U.S. will be over 50 by the year 2000.[14]

☑ The magazine, *Modern Maturity,* has the largest circulation in the U.S. with over 22 million people.[15]

☑ The largest purchasers of vitamins are people over 50 years of age (information from the Tufts Center for the Study of Human Nutrition).

☑ People over 50 years of age purchase the most gourmet foods by mail.[16]

Looking for ways to maintain a comfortable lifestyle during their retirement years, senior citizens are very aware of the returns on their investments. Fluctuations in the economy brought on by a recession or a depression are real threats to their financial security. With older age, comes the threat of ill health and high medical expenses. Adequate health insurance is a priority in many senior citizens' financial planning. Not wanting to be dependent upon others in case of health problems, they will make specific provisions concerning their health care.

[12] Kremer, John, 1001 Ways To Market Your Book, 1989, Ad-Lib Publications, Fairfield, Iowa, 27.

[13] Levinson, Jay Conrad, Guerilla Marketing Attack, 1989, Houghton Mifflin Co., Boston, MA, 144.

[14] Kremer, 27.

[15] Levinson, 145.

[16] Kremer, 27.

Wanting independence in spirit, and good health, they also want the financial flexibility to provide money for their spouse and/or children.

At the other end of the spectrum, we find the senior citizen living on a bare minimum of needs. Having no pension, renting their living quarters with social security as their only source of income, they, too, are targets for a fraud. Even though they have less money than their higher economic counterparts, they are still susceptible to scam artists.

Today, we see more men and women living in seclusion. Whether they find their children living miles away or their neighborhood changing, family members and friendly neighbors may move away and often aren't replaced with another concerned person. There is a great sense of loneliness as they have extra time on their hands. Having no one to talk to or no one who cares often sets the stage for a friendly, smiling face with a willing ear who has other motives in mind. These lonely people may find their suspicions dissolving when an active interest is taken in them. The price of loneliness can have severe consequences. Many people who are isolated and live alone have been befriended and then swindled out of their life savings.

Widowhood is another area of unsuspecting abuse. Because of the woman's reliance upon her deceased husband's decisions concerning business and financial choices, she is open to new outside influences due to her own lack of expertise in these matters. Uncomfortable with the new role thrust upon her and vulnerable soon after his death, she may irrationally believe a stranger will make the same wise decisions her husband once did. Playing to her insecurity and neediness, the con man is a master at the game of deceit. Courting the widow with patience and determination, he slowly gains her confidence. Suddenly, family and friends find their own influence waning under the domination of a "new" advisor.

EVERYBODY'S
BEST FRIEND

•Friendly Persuasion•

Let's look at a couple of scenarios of the con man and senior citizen in action:

Take, for example, the financially secure older American. This gentleman is a man of the world, well-versed about business and the economy. Until retirement, he was deeply involved in civic affairs. He has been retired for several years and is no longer as up-to-date on the business community as he once used to be.

A friend of this gentleman recently introduced him to an astute young man noted to be a whiz at making money for his clients. Upon meeting this young man, the older gentleman was put completely at ease by the younger man's respect and flattery. The con man, disguised as a knowledgeable business advisor, simply stroked the older man's ego. Playing the innocent, the con man gained a quick step in trust with his eager interest and questions about the older man's worldly experience.

As the scene developed, the con man asked for the older gentleman's advice, and then slowly introduced his own risk-free investment. Stoking the fires of a common interest, the con man presented the retired executive with a packet of facts and figures including a bottom-line strategy. Banking on the older man's interest, the con man had studied and researched his plan with full-scale features, advantages, and benefits. He had all the right answers to any objections that the older man might have.

The con man repeatedly pointed out how much more money he could make for the executive than what the gentleman was currently earning on his present investments. Mentioning the fact that his investment was low-risk with high returns, the con man set the stage for the final commitment. Appealing with graphs, columns of numbers, and instinctively playing to the older man's fear of a possible downturn in the economy, the retired executive bought the program hook, line and sinker.

The carefully orchestrated plan worked once again for the con man. He knew exactly what emotional strings to pull. It had worked time and time again. A youthful passion, a beguiling smile, and a reverence for the older gentleman's experience, all disguised his polished performance.

In the same community, we find an older woman who was visiting with a charming and well-mannered young man. This man was listening intently to all of her woes concerning the problems of her recent widowhood. He seemed so understanding and concerned that she asked him to stay for dinner. While dinner was a complete success and she was feeling happier than she had felt in months, our con man introduced a brand-new investment opportunity to her during dessert.

Appealing to the convenience and comfort of doing business with her at her home, she readily agreed that she would appreciate his superior knowledge and service regarding investment opportunities. With merriment in her voice, she said, "I have all this money just sitting around, and I know my husband Harry has sent you to me to tell me what to do with it." The con man cleverly said to her, "God works in mysterious ways." It was goodbye to her timidity, innocence, and money. Once again, a stranger's interest and undivided attention worked wonders in generating her trust.

With quick access to newspapers, it is easy for the con artist to keep track of any recent deaths by reading the obituary notices. Keeping track of new marriage licenses issued helps target a specialty group for the con artist. Watching for winners of the lotto or lottery provides other likely candidates.

Staying within easy reach of the retirement communities, the scam artist can present a very trusting and honorable presence. All he needs is a personal referral to open another door. Milking relationships for investments, he can zero in on several people at once with his wonderful double-digit returns. Building a budding rapport, he promises fantastic returns until he closes the sale. As soon as the older American falls for it, the con man is gone and so, too, is his customer's money.

Today's world is different from the more trusting and secure world of the past. You must be suspicious and skeptical. No matter how comfortable and confident you may feel, do not let your guard down. You never know if the new acquaintence or financial advisor is a friend or foe. The con man is a first-rate actor ready to convince an unsuspecting person of his authenticity.

The use of the telephone is the single most-effective way for the con man to reach his prospect. Whether his call is made locally or comes from out of state, this salesman's talent is to keep you talking. The more he has you talk, the more useful information he learns about you. Geared to stimulating his listener, he pulls you right in with his sales hype and his finely-tuned skills of persuasion. Not wanting to appear rude to this friendly and disarming salesman, many older Americans will not interrupt the phone call or end the conversation. Finding it especially difficult to say goodbye, the senior citizen also finds the con man won't take no for an answer.

Other older Americans find a similar set-up at their doorstep. Finding the salesman so kind and professional, some seniors open their doors to total strangers and welcome them into their homes. Unfortunately, the goodwill of the past has been replaced with a need to be very selective about who we wish to see and talk to about business offers.

For a better idea on what happens to people, let me recreate a few scenes for you. Remember, all these people thought, "this could never happen to me." You, on the other hand, have the information about these stories to help guide you so that you don't end up being another scam statistic. **Be careful, as many times the most innocent approaches may be screens for the most sophisticated scams.**

•Play It Again, Sam•
Split My Winnings
•An elderly woman in Florida was approached by a nice looking lady with a foreign accent. She told the older woman that she had purchased a winning lotto ticket but couldn't cash it as she was an illegal alien. She needed to be a U.S. citizen in order to cash the winning ticket. She showed the older woman the winning ticket as well as the newspaper from the day before verifying the winning numbers. She was a $10,000 winner. If the older woman would help her, then she would be glad to share her winnings. All that was required of the older woman was to pay her one-half of the prize winnings in cash. Then she would give the older woman the winning ticket. The older woman could turn it in and receive the total cash prize. The older woman agreed. She went to her bank and withdrew $5,000. She gave the money to the other lady, and was given the winning ticket in return. When the older woman tried to cash the winning lottery ticket, she was told it was a counterfeit ticket and worthless. Her money was gone.

* * * * * * * *

You're a Winner
•A couple in California received a postcard stating they had won a luxury automobile. Upon calling the company on its toll-free 800 number, it was verified that they were the winners of the luxury automobile. All they had to do to receive their prize was to pay the $1,000 delivery and handling fees. The company would send them a package including their keys and the

information on where they could pick up their new automobile. They were to pay the $1,000 C.O.D. charges on this package with a money order or cashier's check. Then the new luxury car would be theirs. The couple eagerly followed the directions. When the package arrived, it felt like the keys and papers were enclosed. They paid the money and opened the package. All that was inside the package were some key blanks and some torn up newspaper.

* * * * * * * * *

It's So Easy

•A couple from Virginia saw an advertisement in a magazine for a new business opportunity. This venture was investing in public, coin-operated fax machines. The company involved promised to locate the machines in high-traffic areas, maintain them, and send the investors their earnings. It was promoted as an easy, low-risk, high-return investment. For only $25,000, they could purchase ten coin operated fax machines. The couple decided to make the investment. After investing, they did not hear from this company for several months. The couple checked with the company who assured them everything was fine but was just going slower than planned. Six months later, they were especially suspicious. Since this company was located in another state, they decided to hire a private investigator to check out the situation. Through the investigation, the couple found the company had not placed one of the fax machines. The company was suddenly out of business. Their investment was lost.

* * * * * * * * *

Donations, Donations

•A woman in Iowa contributed over $25,000 for several years to what she thought was her political party. She finally decided to check out the individual soliciting the contributions to find out if her money was going to the right organization. Through her investigations, she found out that this person was using a very similar name to a legitimate political organization in order to solicit contributions, and had used the money he raised for his own purposes. Her money was lost. The offender was eventually charged with fraud.

* * * * * * * * *

Pressure Cooker

•A woman living in a retirement community was called by a man representing a retirement organization that sounded official. The name of this organization was similar to another very reputable company. The man wanted to talk to her about the benefits of his organization. He made an appointment and when he stopped by, he started selling her on supplemental nursing home insurance. When he finished his sales pitch, she said no, she was not interested. She asked him to leave, but he continued to stay and pressure her for a decision. After over three hours, being very frustrated and weary, the woman finally agreed to purchase a policy. She wrote out a check for $1,500, and the salesman gave her the policy and left. Later, when one of her children decided to check out the policy and company, it was found to be worthless and non-existent.

* * * * * * * * *

New Technology Craze

•A man was very interested in the new wireless cable technology. Spotting an ad in the newspaper about this a new opportunity, he called the company. It would cost him $5,000 for a license application. He was told that the company had pinpointed the best markets, and a license could be worth several hundred thousand dollars. Obtaining a license was by lottery through a governmental agency. Since it was such a new opportunity, the company assured him that he would be able to obtain a license. He was excited and decided to pay his money. Three months later he had heard nothing from the company, and when he called, the company's phone had been disconnected. His investment was "down the drain."

$$* * * * * * * *$$

Perhaps a simple rule many of our parents taught us as children, **"Don't talk to strangers!,"** might have helped the people in the preceding stories avoid monetary losses and the accompanying headaches. By just following this rule, you can save yourself a lot of aggravation and money.

•He's Got the Whole World in His Hands•

Seniors, you can be a formidable force in the prevention of fraudulent abuse. Your strength lies in your numbers, your purchasing power, your votes, and your well-seasoned life experiences. You have the power to change elected officials, lobby for new laws, and establish new mandates or policies.

As individuals, you can establish phone networks, contact community centers with news of neighborhood alerts, create nerve centers for communication, and set up outreach programs to isolated citizens living alone. You represent a direct link with the heartbeat of the community. And as a group, you offer a powerful coalition for change. Knowledge is the link to the prevention of scams. **To be well-informed is to be well-armed!**

---

6 Common Sense Guidelines for Older Americans:
1) **Do not trust anyone you do not know.**
2) **Be very skeptical and suspicious of all offers.**
3) **Be very analytical and careful when checking out all offers.**
4) **Do not let strangers into your home.**
5) **Do not give out any of your credit card numbers or other personal account numbers to strangers.**
6) **Tell all strange telephone callers that you accept no phone solicitations.**

Seniors, you have the power. You do not have to be another scam statistic. By following these common sense guidelines, you will protect yourselves against scams. (For more information, refer to Chapter 16, p. 139, "Five Easy Rules for Avoiding Scams.")

Next: Seniors Beware

18

Seniors Beware

> *"Where large sums of money are concerned,*
> *it is advisable to trust nobody."*
> Agatha Christie

•Who's Afraid of the Big, Bad Wolf?•

The most prevalent scams that face the older American today are listed here:

•<u>Bank Examiner Scheme</u>•

Several different variations of this scam have been used for years. The con man calls the prospect who he knows as a customer of a particular bank. He identifies himself as an officer of the bank. He flatters the prospect by telling her that he appreciates her loyalty as a good customer of the bank. The officer says the bank has a possible problem with one of its tellers giving out counterfeit bills in exchange for real ones. He wonders if the prospect could be a good citizen and help the bank catch this person in action. All she would have to do is withdraw a specified amount of cash. The officer of the bank would then step in and take the withdrawal as evidence and give her immediate credit for her withdrawal. In reality, there is no credit for the withdrawal and the money disappears. **Who can you trust when it comes to your money?**

•Credit Card Schemes•

These are especially prevalent today. The caller will guarantee you a credit card for a front-end fee or try to give you a good enough reason so you will state your credit card number over the phone. **Do not pay any advance fees nor make your card numbers available to anyone.**

•Direct Debit From Checking Accounts•

This is a relatively new scam. When you decide to purchase an item, you may be told there is a new, simpler method of payment. All that is required of you is to give your bank's name and your checking account number for a direct debit from your account. Later, unauthorized withdrawals may appear on your checking account using counterfeit checks. **Say no to this type of payment.**

•Emergency Alert Devices•

These devices are sold on television using infomercials, on radio, by direct mail, and by magazine ads. This device signals that you need help in an emergency situation. The price tends to be quite high. You can lease an emergency alert device for as little as $10 per month from your local hospital. **Make sure you do some comparative price-shopping by phone.**

•Equity-Skimming Schemes•

These scams can threaten you with the loss of your home as well as your credit rating. Con men may use several different schemes in order to talk you out of the equity in your home or to find a way to borrow against your equity. This can happen to people who are in financial trouble and need a quick sale of their home. Also be wary of being pressured to borrow against your equity or to take out a second mortgage in order to make an investment.

Here are two examples of how equity-skimming schemes work:

In the first example, the con man promises to take over the mortgage payments on your home and make any back payments that are necessary. When the seller signs over the deed and moves out, the con man rents out your home and never assumes the loan or makes any mortage payments. Eventually, the mortgage company begins foreclosure proceedings against you.

A second example involves seniors whose homes are free and clear and listed for sale by the owner. The con man offers to purchase your home at the full asking price. The buyer suggests, in order to make things easier, you use a real estate contract that includes a clause that states the sale is **"subject to a rehabilitation loan."** This clause allows the buyer to go to a lender and borrow money using the equity in the your home as collateral. The buyer borrows the money, and you end up owning and owing on a new mortgage. (When it involves signing over your equity, many states have a three day right of recision so the you can change your mind. Check with your own State Attorney General's office.)

Never sign over your deed or assign your equity to anyone. Always get legal advice first!

•Fake Retirement Associations•

The person who contacts you uses a name for his retirement association that is very similar to an established one. All he really wants to do is get his foot in your door so he can sell you a worthless supplemental health insurance policy or some other product or service you do not need.

•Fundraising, Non-Profits, and Religious Schemes•

There is all kinds of fraud involved in fundraising. It is popular to use words such as "Cancer" or "AIDS" in conjunction with a phony non-profit organization's name. This way, it is much easire to solicit donations. Some may even say you have won a prize if you will give a donation. Don't hesitate to ask what percentage of your donation actually is used for helping the cause and how much is used for the organization's overhead and administration costs. It is important that you know the quality of your religious, charitable, or non-profit organizations before investing. Do not hesitate to write or call for information about non-profits to one of the organizations listed in Chapter 15. **Make sure you ask the organization for its annual report and externally audited financial statement. Be inquisitive!**

•Funeral or Mortuary Programs or Plots•

Seniors are especially vulnerable. These appeal to making your funeral plans in advance or puchasing a burial plot. You pay your money, and end up with nothing in return. **Ask for references first.**

•Health Care Fraud•

Seniors beware. Watch out for calls promising free health checkups or health tests. Be suspicious of anything that is free. Check all your health care bills very carefully. Don't trust anyone trying to sell you on health care services or equipment that your own doctor has not mentioned or is not needed. Con men will not hesitate to use your Medicaid or Medicare numbers to fraudulently bill governmental agencies. **Medicare's toll-free "Fraud Hotline" is 1-800-368-5779. Do not give strangers any of your insurance account numbers, your**

medical history, or any other insurance information.

•Health Products•

Seniors, the main premise here is to sell you products that will make you look younger and stay healthier. Popular products include weight loss programs, arthritis remedies, baldness products, vitamin and mineral supplements, skin care products, and nutrition schemes. Most are overpriced and usually do not work. **Be wary of any newly advertised health products.**

•Hearing Aids•

These are sold with a warranty or money-back refund. Many are poorly made products and do not operate properly. The warranty may not be real, and there is no refund. **Make sure you know your company or product.**

•Home Based Businesses•

Many older Americans who are on fixed incomes may be looking for work they can do at home to add to their incomes. Examples would be making crafts, putting gift items together, or stuffing envelopes.

Usually, you are required to purchase overpriced materials to use to make the products. The company promises that it will purchase your completed items. What you find after finishing the products is that the company is no longer interested in buying them from you. Your investment is gone, and you are left with cheap, worthless materials.

Stay away from ads promoting informational booklets or brochures on subjects such as "How to make money at home" or "How to get rich quickly," etc. They are usually not worth the money you paid for them. **Be skeptical!**

•Home Improvements•

Con men use this ploy to rip-off unsuspecting seniors for large amounts of money every year. Watch out for itinerant crews of roofers, concrete repair, handi-work, etc. Do not pay your money up-front or in advance of the service being provided. You cannot be careful enough when dealing with these people. After the workers have completed their work, check all your window and door locks as they can unlatch a window or door and later burgarlize your home. Be on the lookout for free furnace or roofing inspections, exterminator services, and foundation or driveway repairs. **Ask for references. Beware of all unsolicited workers. Never let strangers into your home!**

•Investment Schemes•

Seniors can be especially susceptible to investment scams that promise to increase the rate of return on their money. These investments usually promise or guarantee high rates of return with low risks. Examples could be gold mines, oil and gas leases or drilling programs, collectibles such as gemstones and coins, and investment funds or real estate partnerships. **Do not hesitate to ask for advice from respected friends or other advisors. Be cautious.**

•Living Trusts•

This involves the sale of living trusts and usually targets the older American. The premise of a living trust is to hold the ownership of your assets during your lifetime and provide for the distribution of those assets at the time of your death. The salesman uses fear or scare tactics playing on your emotions. He tells you a living trust is necessary for your estate so that you will be able to save money, stay out of court, and keep your estate from ending up in the wrong hands. These living trusts are usually written on a generic form which doesn't take into account an individual's specific needs or situation. A living trust may be unnecessary. (Estates with a value of $600,000 or under are usually not subject to probate.) Living trusts written on these generic forms could be contested so you could end up in court. **If you need more advice, call your state government's listing under estate taxes, or a probate/estate attorney.**

•Magazine Subscriptions•

The premise is to offer magazine subscriptions free or at low rates. The free subscriptions include a service fee. The paid subscriptions may be for several years. You usually end up paying far more than you thought you would. Ask for written information on the offer. **Read all the fine print carefully. Your best bet is to say no to these types of deceptive offers.**

•Money Manager or Financial Planner•

These companies and individuals will not hesitate to take your money on the premise of investing your money in various low-risk and high-return investment opportunities. **Thoroughly investigate these people and companies and ask for references.**

•Phone Card Schemes•

The scam artist calls saying he is with your long-distance company, and he would like to verify your long-distance calling card number. Once you give it to him, he may make unauthorized calls against your card. If this happens to you, notify your long-distance carrier immediately and cancel your card. To be on the safe side, tell the caller that you will not give out your card number over the phone. Follow this up with a call to your long-distance company with a complaint. Refuse to give your card number over the phone. When using a pay phone or your calling card in a public place, make sure you do not let anyone see your card's number. **Keep your phone card number to yourself.**

•Phony Foreign Banking Schemes•

Since so many of our banks and savings and loans have had financial problems, you may be wondering where to place your money. These foreign banks sell you on the fact that they can offer you higher returns on your money at less risk. **Don't believe it!**

•"Scavenger" or "Revenge" Scheme•

Seniors are vulnerable to this kind of scam. The company that ripped you off in the past calls on the phone or sends a postcard using a different company's name. You are asked if you would like to put the unethical company out of business and possibly get your money returned. All that is required of you is to pay a specified amount of money to help this new organization fund their investigation and lawsuit in your behalf. Ask for references and more written information. **Hold on to your money!**

•Senior Fear Schemes•

The appeal of these scams is to protect your social security, Medicaid, and other benefits by giving donations to an organization that will lobby in your behalf (ex. social security protection bureau). The con man wants to make you fearful stating that you could lose important benefits. These organizations generally do not exist. Make sure you ask him to send you his organization's brochure and an audited financial statement. Check to find out whether the organization is legitimate. **Always do your homework before making a decision.**

•Supplemental Health Insurance•

These insurance rip-offs offer useless supplemental health insurance policies. Investigate out the company before you sign up. You could end up owning a worthless policy at that critical time when you need to file a claim. Do not feel pressured into making an impulsive decision. **Be clever and calculating.**

•Sweepstakes or Prize Giveaways•

These scams seem to be the most appealing to seniors. Everyone loves to win a free prize, but remember, these offers are not free. Giveaways have strings attached in order for you to receive your prize. A fraudulent sweepstakes company could use a name and printed promotional information that looks similar to a more well-known, legitimate company.

You could be told you have won a cash prize or a luxury gift item. Normally, you are required to pay money or make some kind of purchase first. Sometimes, you are sent an official-looking check made payable to your name. The check or cash prize could be paid to you in coupons, products, or bonds which have little cash value.

If you purchase a product, it is overpriced. There is also a high probability you will never receive your prize. If you do, the prize will not be not what you expected and has little value. And if you win a trip, there could be many restrictions and hidden costs.

Ask for more written information, company financial statements, and references. **Read the fine print carefully.** Generally nothing is free. These offers include exceptions, restrictions or requirements. **Don't let the allure of these prize offers control your rational thinking.**

Obviously, the senior citizen may come into contact with almost any type of scam. For additional information, refer to the "Dictionary of Scams," Chapter 7, page 55.

Next: The Questionnaire: A Risk-Taking Probability Quotient

PART FIVE
The
Final
Analysis

19

The Questionnaire:
(A Risk-Taking Probability Quotient)

•Wheel of Fortune•

Take this questionnaire and find out how vulnerable you are to an investment scam.

1) You are called by a friend who tells you about a fantastic investment opportunity in a computer company which will earn you a much higher than normal return on your money. Your friend knows of no other investment that can compare to this one. He believes this investment is very low-risk because it is secured against a product which has already been produced. Best of all, he says the computer company has future sales contracts which have been negotiated and signed.

    a) You decide to sign up immediately.

    b) Your interest is piqued but being a prudent investor, you ask him for more information on this investment.

    c) You say you are not interested.

2) Your friend calls back and tells you of other acquaintances of yours who have invested their money in this wonderful

opportunity. He says he has already received some incredible returns on his own investment (from 2% to 4% a week). You call some these of other people to verify the news. Each one tells you not to pass up this wonderful investment opportunity.

    a) You decide to sign up immediately.

    b) You still think you need more information on this investment.

    c) You say you are not interested.

3)   Your friend provides you with an audited financial statement on the company. It looks great. You see that this company has a proven track record of success and has been in business for several years.

    a) You decide to go for it.

    b) You are still suspicious and ask for more information.

    c) You remain uninterested.

4)   You go visit the company's offices and find the operation very legitimate. When you meet the president, you like him right away. The president shows you the computers, and tells you that orders are now being shipped to foreign countries. You look at the warehouse, and it is filled with many boxes of computer equipment ready for shipment. You leave feeling very impressed with the company's management and operation.

    a) You decide to go back and sign up.

    b) You are very positive, but still not ready to take the step.

    c) You are still skeptical.

5) Since you are looking for various ways to invest your money, you go to a local investment seminar. The computer company is mentioned and highly recommended as the very best, high-

return/low-risk investment available today.
   a) You can't wait to sign up.
   b) You think maybe you should go ahead but still hesitate on taking the risk.
   c) You decide "no way."

6) You go to church on Sunday. Afterwards, many of the congregation are talking excitedly about this same business investment. A large number of members have already invested. You also learn that the church has invested a large sum of its own money.
   a) Now you can't wait to get your money and to sign the papers.
   b) You are leaning toward making the investment.
   c) It is still "no go."

7) You call your local banker and ask him for his advice on this investment opportunity. He says the computer company has a good business relationship with the bank. He believes the computer company is very stable. He would definitely recommend the investment .
   a) This clinches your decision. You call the president to set an appointment so you can stop by and sign up.
   b) You just cannot make up your mind.
   c) Your gut feelings tell you not to invest.

8) You call the company and talk to the president. He tells you that a local savings and loan has made them a loan of several million dollars. You call the savings and loan and verify what you were told. The S&L also recommends this excellent low-risk investment opportunity.
   a) You have decided to go ahead and enlarge the amount of your investment in order to increase your return.

b) You like the investment but are still procrastinating.

c) You decide a final no on this investment.

Grade yourself based on the following point system:

1) Three points for each a) decision;

2) Two points for each b) decision;

3) One point for each c) decision.

If you score from 17 to 24 points, you are a born risk-taker, and are a likely choice to be caught by a scam.

If you score 9 to 16, you are still willing to take some chances. With a good enough sounding opportunity, you probably could be persuaded to go ahead.

If you score 8 or less, you are conservative, not a risk-taker, and not likely to get caught by a scam.

The above questions were all hypothetical, but were based on one of the largest "Ponzi" schemes ever uncovered. This scam actually took place in Westminster, Colorado (located near Denver and Boulder). It came to the public's attention in 1991.

This interesting fraud involved a company called M&L Business Machines. M&L conned more than 500 investors nationwide out of approximately $25 million. Investors were promised much higher than normal interest rate returns on their money. The money invested with M&L Business Machines was used to help finance the costs of their computer sales operation. M&L supposedly had signed contracts to ship computers to many businesses and foreign countries. It turned out that the boxes of computers in M&L's warehouse were filled with bricks, dirt, and foam. The audited financial statements of M&L were fakes, and M&L had actually avoided paying taxes for several years.

M&L operated this highly polished and sophisticated scam

for over five years. It was a "ponzi" scheme whereby the older investors were paid by new investors' money. Because of the large number of investors involved, many new ones came aboard through personal recommendations.

Capitol Federal Savings loaned M&L $6 million to help finance their operation. Capitol Federal Savings is now bankrupt. A Boulder bank was also involved. It is facing a possible lawsuit.

The scheme began to fall apart when the Securities Division of Colorado started investigating M&L because it offered much higher than normal interest rate returns to private investors. Capitol Federal Savings also called in their own private investigator to check out questions regarding the company. M&L has now filed for protection under Chapter 11 of the Federal Bankruptcy Code. The case is under investigation and charges are pending against the owners.

Was there a major factor that should have given away this scam to the average investor? Yes, it was the **"Greed Factor"** because the return on the investment was **"too good to be true."** (This return on investment was reported to be as high as 2% to 4% a week.) The majority of investors were thinking about how much money they could earn on this investment opportunity. The **"Ease and Time Factors"** (Chapter 11, The Factors, page 98) also played a part in each person's decision to invest with M&L Business Machines.

One final point needs to be made. The testimonials or endorsements from family, friends, and business associates were especially instrumental in each person's decision-making process.

Next: The Ultimate Responsibility

20

The Ultimate Responsibility

> *"Never doubt that a small group of thoughtful,
> committed citizens can change the world;
> indeed, it's the only thing that ever has."*
> Margaret Mead

•It Is Up to Us•

Every person is responsible for the commitment he or she makes. Whether that commitment involves signing a contract or buying a product, we are the ones who sanction the act. If we are well-informed, skeptical of the motives behind the person or the company advertising "too good to be true" possibilities, we are way ahead of the vast majority of people. Too often times, we let our emotional nature outweigh our rational analysis.

Look at the ease in which credit cards are extended to people and the amount of running debt that is incurred by the quick, impulsive purchasing power. Building upon the premise of a quick fix, people have learned to pacify their emotional needs with investments. Enticing people into fraudulent investments by appealing to their emotional needs has been increasingly successful for the company scam.

175

Where will the line be drawn? How do we stop this growing industry corrupting our faith and trust in our fellow man? **The ultimate responsibility comes back to each one of us.**

•Making a Difference•

First, we must understand that when we sign on the dotted line or give approval to use our credit card number, we give permission and have to deal with all the consequences. I believe one way people learn to say no is from personal experience. Whether it is one's own personal story or someone elses, you know of, these shared stories have a moral. Telling these tales of woe lifts the burden of the mistake and creates a desire to learn from it.

Learning to say no may take a few hard lessons, but "the school of hard knocks" has quite a few success stories. Your mistake may save another person from repeating the same one. When you multiply one person's awareness by many, the number of successes by the con artist diminishes. Suddenly, the con man loses his power. One person's story may expand into many supporting stories. Breaking the silence casts the first blow against this power of corruption.

Today, we are living in a high tech world of instant communications. When people hear through the media of a specific scam occurring in their city, they become much more cautious. In only a few seconds, one story can be broadcast around the world.

•When Sally Met•

Visualize the following scenario and the power of exposure for Sally Day:

Sally Day lost $5,000 to an out-of-state company selling cosmetics. She paid her money and never received her product from the company. When she called the cosmetic company, she was told the product was back-ordered. After repeated long-distance calls at her own expense (the company did not have a toll free 800 number), she continued to get excuses.

Sally was outraged and told her neighbor the story. The neighbor called her husband's cousin who worked at a local television station. The cousin mentioned Sally's story during his Monday sales meeting. Her story generated immediate interest. She gained empathy and support from a news team she did not know. A reporter and camera crew were sent to Sally's home for an interview. The station decided to air Sally's story under a "Consumer Awareness" segment. The night the story was aired, the station's switchboard lit up. Sally, it seems, was not the only one who had lost money to this cosmetic company. Five more people came forward to corroborate Sally's story.

A follow-up news story ran four nights later with interviews with the other five unhappy consumers. An affiliated TV station located in the cosmetic company's city also broadcast the program featuring Sally and the followup interviews with the other five consumers. In the meantime, the news crew working on Sally's story was sent to interview the cosmetic company located out of state. The cosmetic company refused to talk to anyone. The bad press had already damaged the cosmetic company's reputation.

Sally, at the same time, had been asked by a production manager at a local radio station to appear on a talk show program entitled, "Citizen's Alert." While appearing on this talk radio show, Sally was advised to contact the State Attorney's office in the state where the cosmetic company was located. When she called a fellow in the consumer fraud division of the State Attorney's office, Sally was told that the cosmetic company was already under investigation. She was advised to send a formal letter of complaint to the State Attorney's office. It was also suggested to Sally that she ask the other unhappy consumers to do likewise, as it would help strengthen the investigation.

The power of communication continued to ripple outward and expand. Suddenly, the story which was told to Sally's neighbor had become a major news story overnight. The offender, whether a person or company, no longer had invisible power. The victim was seen and supported while the culprit was exposed. Public awareness created the perfect forum to fight back. In the past, keeping silent would had given this scam a good name.

Incidently, the whole story on Sally continues to grow. Several months later, she was seen at the state capitol meeting with a few legislators discussing the need for stronger legislation to protect the consumer. Sally, you see, is no different from you and me. She is an average American citizen who spoke out and made a difference. We can accomplish similar results.

•Word of Mouth•

There are many methods of speaking out against this formidable force of greed and deception. One voice multiplied by many has countless avenues for expression. Contact the proper agencies and file a complaint. Communication to our citizens by means of newsletters, editorials, talk radio, toll-free information "hot lines," computer clubs, various associations, TV programs, etc. spreads the word.

Injustice needs to be voiced. That same injustice often gets billed as foolish mistakes. Voicing our mistakes lifts each personal story from a first-hand experience to "there are others out there who have made similar mistakes." We are all human. Understanding and analyzing what we did wrong gives us more power over the incident. Insight does heal! It also provides clues to make sure we stop the mistakes from becoming a repetitive pattern.

The real key to taking the power away from the abuser of trust and ethics is to speak out against him! Awareness of specific frauds happening in a person's community arms that citizen with the knowledge of the abuser and the ability to say no.

For more information on "Who to Call for Help?," refer to Chapter 15, page 125. The next chapter includes a newsletter format as a creative example of how to communicate the latest information.

Next: Points of Power Newsletter

21

Creating the Forum to Fight Fraud

Points of Power Newsletter

Issue No. 1, Page 1

7 Tools for Influencing Others

1. Newsletters
2. Direct Mailing
3. Media Releases
4. Newspaper Advertising
5. Radio and Television
6. Telephone Networking
7. Clubs and Associations

New Toll-Free Fraud Hotline available soon--to be called "Natl. Fraud Information Center"

The National Consumers League estimates telemarketing fraud has now gone over $15 billion in annual losses. The National Consumer League announced that there will be a 1-800-Fraud Hotline. City Bank, MCI, and MasterCard are just a few of the major companies who have agreed to help under-

> *"The best way to find a solution to your problems is to help others solve theirs."*
> Unknown

write such an important project. The new toll-free hotline number is listed as **1-800-876-7060** and is called the **National Fraud Information Center.**

(Points of Power Newsletter, page 2)
Letters to the Editor:

Dear Sir:

I recently read in The Denver Post that a toll free 1-800 "scam hotline" will soon be available for the consumer's use. As a PC computer owner, I will be able to also access this system by my modem through a bulletin board. I will be able to gather the latest information on scams. To me it is a sign that we are fighting back. We will soon have a new source of information ready to serve the public. Hurray!

Sincerely yours,
Jane Nugent

To whom it may concern:

The amount of information on scams seems to be exploding. I see and hear stories almost daily on the subject. All you have to do is watch your television, listen to the radio, and read your favorite magazines, and newspapers. A media blitz on scams is taking place. The public is not going to continue to be victimized. It is about time we get the word out, and stop these crooks from ripping us off.

Best regards,
Jeff Cutler

To whom it may concern:

I am thrilled to see a number of recent newspaper and television stories about the fight against scams. It is wonderful that these illegal operations are being put out of business and the culprits are being convicted. It also is great to see that there seems to be excellent cooperation taking place among the various investigating law enforcement agencies. Justice will prevail!

Sincerely,
George Jonas

(Points of Power Newsletter, page 3)

> *"Nothing strengthens the judgement and*
> *quickens the conscience like individual responsibility."*
> Elizabeth Cady Stanton

Editorial:

The time has come for the grass roots of America to be heard. The government is crippled with too little help, too little time, and too little authority. We can speak out, take a stand against corruption, and put our money in ethical investments. We can stop these corrupt people and companies by refusing to support them in silence. We are responsible for stopping these abusive practices. We must carefully scrutinize all new offers and opportunities.

Each person can be a point of power. Individuals can attract the attention of many people. One person can make a difference while many people can make a groundswell for change. Filing complaints with the proper agencies and alerting people about the current scams in our vicinity or local area spreads the word.

I believe we are the powerful minority ready to become the majority. Sounding the alarm on deceitful practices arms the public with vital information. We, the citizens, are taking back our power, spreading the word, and fighting back.

I am interested in hearing your unusual stories on winning battles against fraud. If your story is used in my newsletter or follow-up book, I'll send you a free copy of the one in which it appears. Also, if you enjoyed this book or found it beneficial and informative, I would appreciate your comments.

Graham M. Mott, P.O. Box 687, Littleton, CO. 80160, 1-303-797-6116

Next: Afterword

22

Afterword

> "We learn wisdom from failure much more than from success;
> We often discover what will do by finding out what will not do;
> And probably he who never made a mistake never made a discovery."
> Samuel Smiles

•The Never-Ending Story•

This book has had a power all of its own. As I was writing my story, I received affirmations all along the way. The response to the topic has been so favorable and the enthusiasm I received so heartwarming that it made reliving my experiences and mistakes with XYZ Company worthwhile.

Each time I was looking for something, it just seemed to literally fall into my lap. When I needed computer help, there was always a friend available to assist me. When I needed assistance with my cover, I met a graphic artist in a office products store who gave me his free advice. A friend introduced me to other authors, recorded TV shows on scams, and cut out magazine and newspapers articles on the subject. When eating out one weekend, I was introduced to a friend of my son who was a cartoonist. Before I sent the book to the printer, I was able to obtain the toll-free 800 hotline phone number for the

National Fraud Information Center. And there were many other special happenings that all fell into place. It has been a wonderful oddessy writing this book.

As Robert Schuller states so well, "Turn your scars into stars."[17] I did and so can you. Instead of betting on someone else, this time I took a risk on myself.

[17] "c. 1992 Robert H. Schuller, all rights reserved, reprinted with permission."

PART SIX
Appendix

Glossary of Terms

Agent: A person who is authorized to act for or represent another person in dealing with a third party.*

Company-Owned Unit: An outlet owned and operated by the parent company.*

Dealer: A person or firm marketing a product in a specified geological area.*

Distributor: Middleman, wholesaler, agent, or company who distributes goods to dealers or companies.*

Franchise: Requires three elements: 1) franchise fee; 2) common trade name; 3) continuous relationship with the parent company.*

Fraud: A deceit, trickery, an intentional attempt to deprive you of money, property, or a lawful right; a breach of confidence perpetrated for profit.

Independent Contractor: A person or business who represents another company but does so solely with his own business and operating expenses.

Leads: Names, addresses, and/or telephone numbers of potential customers provided to the operator by the parent company.*

Major Distributor: (This type of distributor may be called different names by other companies.) This is the top distributorship level which includes an exclusive protected territory, the right to hire a sales staff, and also to sell other distributors who would work under the Major Distributor. Also this position would include no direct sales competition from the company.

Multi-Level Sales: Also known as network marketing. Rather than hiring a sales staff, multi-level sales companies sell their products through thousands of independent distributors. Multi-level sales companies offer distributors commissions on both retail sales and also on the sales of their "downlines" (the

*These definitions are from "A Glossary of Business Opportunity Terms," Entrepreneur Magazine, July 1992, 144.

network of other distributors they sponsor) plus various bonuses for attaining certain levels of sales and recruitment.*

On Consignment: These are goods shipped or turned over to an agent for sale with payment to the shipper to follow after the sale.*

Operator: An entrepreneur who buys a business opportunity.*

Principal: A person who appoints another to act for him or her as an agent.*

Protected Territory: An exclusive territory granted to the entrepreneur by the parent company in which to sell a product or service.*

Rack Jobber: A wholesaler serving retail stores who selects, assembles, prices, arranges, maintains displays, and delivers merchandise on the dealer's floor. This person sells primarily on a consignment basis.*

Residual or Override Commissions: These are commissions paid on renewal sales or redemptions. These are future sales that are part of or tied to the original sale. These commissions may also be based on a company's earnings or profits.

Retailer: Is a person involved in the final sales to the consumer/user of goods and services. Sells goods in smaller amounts or quantities.*

Scam: A confidence game or other fraudulent scheme for making a profit: to cheat or defraud, a swindle, swindler, swindling.

Scambuster: One who refuses to be victimized; one who speaks out about scams.

Turnkey: This means that everything you need to start a business is provided. Literally, all you have to do is turn the key and you are in business.*

Wholesaler: A merchant middleman who sells to retailers and other commercial users but does not sell in any quantities to the ultimate (end) consumers.*

*These definitions are from "A Glossary of Business Opportunity Terms," Entrepreneur Magazine, July 1992, 144.

Bibliography

The following is a list of books, pamphlets, calendars, magazines, and newpapers that I used to research my book. I would recommend them as excellent reading material.

"A Glossary of Business Terms," Entrepreneur Magazine, July 1992, 144.

Allen, Eugenie and Fretts, Bruce, Forbes 1992 Executive Page-A-Day Calendar, Workman Publishing Co., Inc., New York, NY.

Bates, Dennis G., "Fraud By Mail," Modern Maturity, April-May 1991, 33.

Bekey, Michele, "Dial S-W-I-N-D-L-E," Modern Maturity, April-May 1991, 31-40.

Bowers, Brent, "Small Businesses Increasingly Become Targets of Scams," The Wall Street Journal, January 14, 1992.

Briggs, Bill, "Who Knows Where the Money Goes?," The Denver Post, April 6, 1992, E:1,4.

Buckstein, Caryl, "Job scams can trap consumers," The Denver Post, August 16, 1992, 6H.

Buckstein, Caryl, "Scam artists extend their reach," The Denver Post, August 9, 1992, 8H.

Carnevale, Mary Lu, "Fraud Complaints Grow in Young Wireless Cable Field," The Wall Street Journal, June 24, 1992, B2.

Castro, Janice, "Reach Out And Rob Someone," Time, April 3, 1989, 38.

"Casualties of Fraud," The Denver Post, February 17, 1992, C:1,2.

"Con Games That Target The Elderly," Consumers Research Magazine, September 91, 30-32.

Connor, Chance, "Tracking sports-memorabilia fraud," The Denver Post, H:1,5.

Day, Janet and Robinson, Marilyn, "Indictments allege massive M&L fraud," The Denver Post, February 28, 1992, A:1,9.

Day,Janet, "M&L executives, investors a collage of lifestyles," The Denver Post, March 1,1992, H:16.

Day, Janet, "M&L investment fraud case keeps getting bigger," The Denver Post, February 24, 1991, C:1,2.

Day, Janet, "M&L kingpin denied fraud," The Denver Post, February 29, 1992, A:1,20.

Emshwiller, John R., "Dial 'M' for Misleading Claims of Coin-Operated Riches," The Wall Street Journal, January 15, 1992.

Fifteenth Report by the Committee on Government Operations,The Scourge of Telemarketing Fraud: What Can Be Done Against It?, House Report #102-421, December 18, 1991, U.S. Government Printing Office, Washington, DC.

Fisk, Jim and Barton, Robert, The Official MBA Handbook of Great Business Quotation, 1984, A Fireside Book, Simon and Shuster, Inc., New York, NY.

"For the Unwary Investor, There's a Scam Born Every Minute", Business Week, December 26, 1988, 182.

"Fraudbusters: The Top Ten Scams," Consumers Research Magazine, June 1989, 32.

Gallagher Ph. D., Bill and Wilson, Orval Ray, and Levinson, Jay Conrad, The Guerilla Selling Newsletter, Vol.1 No. 2, The Guerilla Group.

Giorgianni, Anthony, "How do you determine deserving charities?," The Denver Post, April 6, 1992, E:4.

Gottschalk, Earl C. Jr., "Scam Artists Weave Clever New Webs to Entrap the Unsuspecting Investor," The Wall Street Journal, Oct. 23, 1992, C1, C13.

Grossman, Cathy Lynn, "Beware of those cheap selling trips," July 8, 1992, USA Today, 1-2D.

Hamburg, J., "Scam Alert! How to Avoid a Rip-off," Ladies Home Journal, July 1989, 44, 49.

Harris, Marlys, "Fraud," Money, August 1989, 75-80.

Harris, M. J., "You May Already Be A Victim Of Fraud," Money, August 1989, 75.

Hayward, Susan, A Guide for the Advanced Soul, April 1990, Mandarin Offset, HK.;

"Health Care Fraud," U.S. News and World Report, February 24, 1992, 38-50.

"Here's how to spot and stop those sneaky consumer scams," (from Redbook Magazine), The Denver Post, Oct. 6, 1992, 8L.

Hernandez, Raul, "Steer clear of scams when fixing your credit," The El Paso Herald Post, Oct. 7, 1992.

"Infomercials are filling the late-night hours with tacky pitches for everything from kitchen tools to baldness cures," Time, June 17, 1991.

Kremer, John, 1001 Ways to Market Your Books, 1989, Ad-Lib Publications, Fairfield, IA.

Lawlor, Julia, "Job-scam artists work overtime," July 9, 1992, USA Today, 9B.

Levinson, Jay Conrad, Guerilla Marketing Attack, 1989, Houghton Mifflin Company, Boston, MA.

Ley, D. Forbes, The Best Seller, 1990, Sales Successs Press, Newport Beach, California.

McCarroll, Thomas, "Who's Counting?," Time, April 13, 1992, 48-50.

McGovern, Kris, "Invest carefully to avoid scams," The Denver Post, March 22, 1992, H:4.

Paulson, M. C., "You Definitely Have Won A Fabulous Prize!," Changing Times, August 1989, 38-40.

Poynter, Dan, The Self-Publishing Manual, 1989, Para Publishing, Santa Barbara, CA.

Pratkanis, Anthony and Aranson, Elliot, Age of Propaganda, 1992, W. H. Feldman, New York, NY.

Quinn, Jane Bryant, "How to read between insurance company ratings," The Rocky Mountain News, July 21, 1992, B1.

Quinn, Jane Bryant, "This Suit's for Vu," Newsweek, April 13, 1992, 46-47.

Reckard, E. Scott, "Lawsuit alleges vast telemarketing fraud," The Denver Post, August 26, 1992, 8C.

Reiss, S. and Katel, P, "Still A Con Man's Paradise," Newsweek, May 28, 1990.

Romig, Jack, 365 Ways To Save Our Planet, a Page-A-Day calendar, Workman Publishing Co., New York, NY.

Ross, Tom and Marilyn, The Complete Guide to Self-Publishing, 1985, Writer's Digest Books, Cincinnati, Ohio.

Schultz, Ellen E., "Credit Card Crooks Devise New Scams," The Wall Street Journal, July 17, 1992, C:1,2.

Smith, Lindsay, "How Gullible Are You," Modern Maturity, April-May1991, 42-46.

Stern, Richard L. and Abelson, Reed, "The Second Oldest Industry?," Forbes, June 24, 1991, 236.

"Still a Con Man's Paradise," Newsweek, May 28, 1990, 49-50.

"Swindlers Are Calling," an educational brochure, 1990, Alliance Against Fraud in Telemarketing,National Futures Association, Commodity Futures Trading Commission and Federal Trade Commission.

"Telephone Scams for the 1990's," Consumer Research Magazine, May 1990, 29.

The NASAA and Council of BBB, Investor Alert, A Benjamin Book, Andrews and McMeel, February 1988, A Universal Press Syndicate Co.

"The Top Ten Health Frauds," Consumers Research Magazine, February 1990, 34.

Waldman, Steven, "Dial M For Marketing Fraud," Newsweek, May 16, 1988.

Wilmsen, Steven, "Scam victims seek missing millions," The Denver Post, July 12, 1992, 1,12.

Winfield, BiBi, Checkers Moving, 1987, A Fireside Book, Simon and Schuster, Inc.

Woman to Woman, a daily calendar, 1991, Impressions Ink, Inc., Memphis, Tenn.

Zoglin, Richard, "It's amazing! Call now!," Time, June 17, 1992, 71.

Thanks also to all the following agencies and businesses for their help and information:

- American Society of Retired Persons
- American Society of Travel Agents
- Better Business Bureau
- Business Radio Network
- Central Phone Number for Congress
- Colorado State Attorney General's Office
- Commodity Futures Trading Commission
- Consumer Health Information Research Institute
- Denver District Attorney's Office
- Direct Marketing Association
- Dun and Bradstreet
- Environmental Protection Agency
- Federal Trade Commission
- Food and Drug Administration
- Medicare and Medicaid Hotline
- National Association of Securities Dealers
- National Charities Information Bureau
- National Committee for Responsible Philanthropy
- National Consumers League
- National Council Against Health Fraud
- National Fraud Information Center
- National Futures Association
- National Insurance Crime Bureau
- National Insurance Information Institute
- North American Securities Administrators Association
- Philanthropic Advisory Service
- Securities and Exchange Commission
- U.S. Postal Service

Next: Evaluation of an Offer Form and Five Easy Rules for Avoiding Scams (easy-to-use copy pages)

Index

(copy page)

✔An Evaluation of an Offer✔

√This checklist is strictly a guide to use to help you arrive
  at a correct decision.
√Name of compay:_____
√The address:_____
√City, state, zip code:_____
√Phone no:_____
√Date of 1st call:_____
√Name of person:_____
√Who called whom? _____
√What did you talk about?_____
_____

√How did did you hear about the offer?_____
_____

√How long has this company been in business? _____
√How good is this offer? _____
√Are you requesting more information to be mailed to you?
  _____What was the company's attitude?_____
_____

√Will the company provide you with references? (preferrably in your state)_____
  names and phone numbers:_____
_____

√Are you being pressured to sign up or pay with a credit
  card?_____
√Is there any obligation to purchase anything in order to
  receive the offer? _____
√How much do you know about this kind of offer or
  business?_____ Have you read the fine print?___
√Are you being promised things that are "too good to be
  true"? _____ How risky is this offer?_____
√Make sure you always get other opinions from friends,
  business associates, or an attorney.

(copy page)

Five Easy Rules
for Avoiding Scams

Rule #1: **Do not get involved if what you hear or read is "too good to be true," because then it is.**

Rule #2: **Do not purchase or invest money with any person you do not know whether over the phone, in person, or by mail.**

Rule #3: **Do not do business with any company located out of state.**

Rule #4: **Do not invest unless you can afford to lose your investment.**

Rule #5: **Do not give your personal credit card numbers or other personal numbers to a stranger by telephone or by mail.**

*The exception to rules 2, 3, and 5 would occur only if you feel sure you can trust the company or person with whom you are conducting business.

About the Author

Graham M. Mott, author, publisher, real estate broker, investor, fly fisherman, resides with his wife, daughter, and two sons in Littleton, Colorado.

(copy page)

Book Order Form for
How to Recognize and Avoid
Scams, Swindles, and Rip-offs

by Graham M. Mott

Mail the order form below to: **Golden Shadows Press, P.O. Box 687, Littleton, Co. 80160.**

Cost per book: $11.95 plus $4.00 for first class priority mail and handling. For each additional book ordered, add $2.00 each for postage and handling.

Total number of books ordered_____@$11.95 equals $_____

Amount for postage and handling $_____

Add 3.8% Colorado sales tax or $.46 per book for Denver metro residents and 3% or $.36 per book for other Colorado residents $_____

Total amount enclosed $_____

Type of payment (Check one)
____ Check ____ Money Order
MC____Visa ____ Number_____
Expires_____

Cardholder's signature_____

Name _____

Address_____

City _____ State _____ Zip_____

Daytime Phone _____ Evening Phone _____

*All Canadian and foreign orders must be in dollars and include $10 to cover shipping and handling.